Edward Solon Goodhu

Verses from the Valley

Edward Solon Goodhu

Verses from the Valley

ISBN/EAN: 9783744652117

Printed in Europe, USA, Canada, Australia, Japan

Cover: Foto ©Thomas Meinert / pixelio.de

More available books at **www.hansebooks.com**

SUNNYSIDE (pages 67, 90).

VERSES

FROM THE VALLEY.

BY E. S. GOODHUE.

"All are architects of Fate,
  Working in these walls of Time;
Some with massive deeds and great,
  Some with ornaments of rhyme.

"Nothing useless is, or low;
  Each thing in its place is best;
And what seems but idle show
  Strengthens and supports the rest."
—Longfellow.

OAKLAND:
PACIFIC PRESS PUBLISHING COMPANY.
1888.

"O flowering stretches glow and shine,
The language of my heart is thine."

TO HIS DEAR MOTHER

These Verses Are Lovingly Dedicated

BY THE AUTHOR.

RIVERSIDE, AUGUST, 1888.

CONTENTS.

——o——

EARLY PIECES.

---o---

TRANSLATIONS.

---o---

FLORIDIANA.

THY LAND WITH ITS HIGH, HIGH HILLS, AND ITS SUNKEN DALES

MISCELLANEOUS.

—o—

CONSPIRACY.

"THOU comest again?"
Said the mild-faced moon
To the bearded rime,
"Thou comest again?"

"Aye, aye," cried the giant, as hurrying fast
He came from the North in a northern blast,
"I have touched thy land at last.
Thy land with its high, high hills
And its sunken dales;
With its lakes of crystal; with its mountain rills
And its vales.
I shall spread my tent some night
Upon that plain of flowers.
When the sun is asleep and far away,
When you smile upon earth in a silver ray,
I will alight,
And blow my cold breath for hours and hours,
Till the lakes smoke up, and the rills sink low;
Till the hills are covered with inches of snow,
And all the flowers that lie in the vale
Shall utter a wail, and lament and cry:
'Oh! spare us to-night! Oh! let us not die;'
But I shall breathe out my frosty breath
And bring to a million of flowers their death."

"Thou art cruel, O frost!"
Said the kind-faced moon
To the frosty king.
"The North is thy home,
And why shouldst thou roam
To this joyous land where roses blow,
When your land is buried in ice and snow?
Thou art well in thy place,
And thy bearded face,
Frozen with ice into points of glass
Which rattle and glitter as we pass,
Is merry full oft, and kindly withal,
Bringing much cheer to great and to small.

"A month ago in the North, the leaves fell
Down from the trees.
Euroclydon came sandalless and cried:
'Now is the day at hand, come forth!
Prepare ye every one. A knell
Sounds loud in every whistling wind;
Summer and sun and warmth have died.'

"Forthwith the leaves turned red,
The shining silks of corn grew brown,
The pumpkins yellow. Overhead
A sea of leaden sky did drown
The former blue, and cast about
Its waves of drifting cloud,
East, west, and north, and south,
Like vast redoubts
To guard some cannon's mouth.
Rain came, and chilly air,

With winds that shook the apples down,
Now ripe and mellow, plump and brown;
While crows flew southward, flock by flock,
And goose and crane and wily hawk;
Full grew the barns of scented hay,
But every field grew bare and gray.

"Then one night the snow
Came falling down,
And fell into the field and into the town.
Down thro' the darkness, flake by flake,
While the world slept and none were awake.
And when morning came they saw thy face,
It was smiling to them from an open space.
So they cried: 'He has come, he has come,
For the rivers and lakes are stricken dumb.'

"After that night when I looked on the earth,
It was ringing with laughter and mirth;
White were the river and lake;
Buried each bush and brake;
And thine icy breath
Brought life, not death.
Far below, below,
Deep under the snow,
Were hidden the flowers and blades of grass.
And lads were shouting: 'Oh ho! oh ho!
Here is the snow, the snow.'

"As I smile on these flowers to-night,
And the warm wind touches them soft and light.
I smile as well on a different sight:
Far up in the North, on a frozen lake,

Many lads and lassies do gaily make
The country around them in mirth awake.
They are skating and sliding and slipping along,
Hand in hand to the tune of a song,
Muffled and hidden in blanket and fur;
Hidden as safe as a nut in its burr.

"Blow and bluster, King Winter
Freeze the air into ice,
These are ready to greet thee
In any device;
But come not, I pray thee,
To frighten the children
Of sunshine and warmth."

Thus answered the king:
"To-night I shall visit this foot-hill and plain;
To-morrow your sun may well number his slain;
For my mission is hither,
I cannot go back:
Though, alack! alack!
I blight and I wither
The flowers in my track.
I rode from the North on the ridge of your mountain;
In the darkness I came;
And soon all the sleeping
Will rise into weeping."

Then the stars flashed and twinkled
Out into the sky,
And Mars made reply,
"You hard-hearted monster,
Go back to your place,

Where the icicles hang,
Like fruit from the trees,
As they hang from your face.
Go back to your kingdom
And lasting disgrace."

"Tis cold, cold, cold,
I fear I'm growing old,"
Whispered a larkspur trembling.
Then Venus called across the space:
"Come not, O king! be not so base;
Not for one day,
Come not, I pray."

But the old king laughed as he stood on the hill,
Bearded and frozen, with long, hoary locks;
As he shook off the frost from his crimson frill,
And stamped in the snow with his leathern socks.

"Down from the hill I will glide
And slide;
Down to the valley
Through cañon and alley."

At this the stars grew larger, blinking,
And the moon moved swifter on;
A south wind came, and winking
The moon-man's smile was longer drawn,
As from the corners of the sky
Clouds grew and spread afar and nigh,
Huge, black, and swift they hurried by;
Loud from above the thunder pealed;
Moon, stars, and all were now concealed,

While torrents fell
On hill and dell.

—o—

FLOWERS.

O PRECIOUS, precious flowers! I love
Your glad, sweet faces as they smile
Up from the hills for many a mile;
Up to the light which from above
Comes to you, like some white-winged dove,
With cheering message for a while!
Oh! could I longer here beguile
Your shortening stay, and to you prove
How very much I love you all,
And how you fill my heart with joy;
How thoughts go back at your soft call,
To days when I was but a boy,
When, hidden in the blossoms tall,
I did my happy hours employ.

Or, gathering May-buds in the spring—
Under the birch and maple trees—
For wondering boys and busy bees
Left as a graceful offering—
I wreathed around my hat a ring
And there fell down upon my knees,
Thanking the God who all things sees,
In prayer that was a whispering,
For all these tiny tokens fair,
Scattered with such a lavish hand;

For you, dear flowers, who have no care,
  But work in silence through the land!
Then, taking all my arms could bear,
  Went home along the river strand.

    And, as upon the mountain-side
I lie and watch the stretching plain,
Boyhood comes back to me again,
And years among the daisies hide,
As though, sweet years, they had not died.
Old memories loved crowd thro' my brain,
Bringing a sort of spirit-pain—
    With o'ergrown vistas opened wide;
And once again the gratitude
  That filled my child-heart, flowing o'er,
As stood I in the maple-wood,
  Comes down upon me as before,
And to kind Nature's God I would
  My heart in grateful feelings pour.
Pachappa Hill.

——o——

A LESSON.

At my window an apricot tree
  That has stood there the long winter through,
As leafless and bare as a dead thing could be,
  Has taken on robes fresh and new,
And dressed up as gaily as any fair maid,
That comes to the church in her beauty arrayed.

I was thinking not long since—Ah! well,

I will cut down that rough-looking tree,
For I thought, as I heard others tell,
It was really no service to me;
Ungrateful and selfish I was, I confess,
And very forgetful of past kindliness.

Lo! this morning I awoke, and beheld
Every twig clothed in purity white,
A thousand sweet blossoms—six petals each held–
Their faces so happy and bright,
As if to reprove my impatience, and say:
Be less hasty in judging of others, I pray.

'Tis a comfort to me when I sit
And look toward the west, from my room,
To watch how the petals are lit,
As the morning light falls on their bloom;
And I promise my heart ne'er a child shall I be,
But this lesson will learn from my apricot tree:

That each has his work, and his time
In which that same work should be done;
That waiting is labor sublime,
When preparing and waiting are one;
That many adjudged to be idle, are those
Who make the world better, and lessen its woes.

That another I never may chide,
Till I know the intents of his heart;
By God's standard his works may abide,
As my own, by that standard, depart;
That with good-will and patience, results we shall
From men, as from also my apricot tree.

IN THE TULES.

CHATTER and chatter and chatter,
In the tall tules all day long,
Singing a blackbird chorus
To the notes of a blackbird song.

Darker than jet are the singers,
And their coats shine in the sun;
Whistle, and sing, and chatter
Will they till the day is done.

And as long as the moonlight glances
Down into the blades of green;
As long as one ray of glimmer
May over the hills be seen.

Early and bright in the morning,
Ere old Helios calls his steed,
Swinging are all my blackbirds,
On many a flag and reed.

To the music of the clatter,
The cat's-tails nod and bend,
While the small stalks shake and shiver,
Yet attentively attend.

"Oh! fie on these noisy madcaps,"
A fussy old mud-hen cries,
As out, with an angry splutter,
She quick from her snug nest hies.

"How tired am I of such revels,
Such wild and hilarious mirth;

I declare, not one hour have I rested,
  Not one hour since the day of my birth."

And away off she flies, as huffy
  As ever a mud-hen was,
Cursing the birds for her trouble,
  And calling them heartless daws.

Two turtle-doves cooed from the branches;
  Four rabbits were met; "Such a chance,"
Said one of the four to the others,
  "For a giddy whirl and a dance."

'Twas a dance to the blackbird music,
  And much of a rigadoon,
As you might have seen, had you watched them,
  As they danced by the light of the moon.

Chatter and chatter and chatter,
  In the tall tules all day long,
Singing a blackbird chorus,
  At the end of a blackbird song.

——o——

TO P. H. H.

"THERE lives the poet," said he, pointing down
To a low cottage in the oak and pine:
"He who has writ so many a joyous line,"
Then left me on the hill, and to the town
Went slowly back. As through the old trees brown
The morning sunbeams now began to shine,
And flood the forest with their light divine,

I stayed upon the fragrant sward, and sat me down,
Thinking of all thy inspirations sweet,
Caught, poet, from thy happy Southern wood,
Where mocking birds in merry concerts meet,
And sighing pines for centuries have stood.
Then blessed I thee for all thy strains that greet
And cheer the hearts of men, with weary feet.
Here could I praises sing, and fondly tell
Unto my soul and to the aged trees;
To blades of grass and birds and humble-bees,
Words they might list and understand as well,
But which, if in thine ear they sounding fell,
Would grate thee and thy poet's soul displease.

Augusta, Ga., October, 1881.

——o——

MY VALLEY.

My valley hidden lies
  Within its circling hills,
Above it stretch the arching skies,
  And to it Northern chills,
Ne'er come with deadly breath to freeze,
The life-blood of its orange trees.

Italian skies smile down
  Upon the reaching plain,
Where glossy groves of far renown,
  Hang with the fruit of Spain;
Praised oft with poet's fire and zest,
The golden apples of the west—

Fruit given to Jupiter,
  The highest god, by one
Who, queen of heaven, possessed in her
  The beauty of the sun—
Small spheres of gold which tempting shine
Like rounded nuggets of the mine.

Armenia's children spread
  Their ovate foliage wide,
And pomegranate blossoms red
  Behind the hedges hide;
Australian giants, odd and tall,
Stretch awkward branches over all.

I love my valley, and
  I love what in it lies;
Not only miles of beauteous land
  And cloudless, smiling skies,
But hearts of many there, who hold
The love I treasure more than gold.

They love my valley too,
  For theirs it is as well.
And sheltered 'neath its dome of blue
  In fairy homes they dwell.
Olympian gods might envy those
Who in my vale find their repose.

Riverside, Cal.

——o——

ECHO CASTLE.

AGAIN I see a castle old,
With broken gate and shattered tower,
Covered with vines of passion-flower.

Alone it stood among the oak
And palm and bay trees, deep in gloom,
With windows high and spacious room.

Not far away the ocean tossed
Its noisy wave against a shore,
That lay resistant in the roar,

And groaned in deep-toned voice, around
The castle and through all the wood,
As only earth to ocean could.

Here came we when the sun went down,
And from the west a reddening glow
Fell upon us and all below,

Touching the trees with darker shade.
Tinting the white blooms as they lay
Closing almost, at close of day.

"Come, let us go within," I said,
And climb the stairway of the tower,
There to enjoy our leisure hour.

And so through darksome hall we went,
Yet pausing oft to catch the sound
That from our footsteps echoed round.

"Alice," the echo ever cried,
From sound of voice or footstep fall,
"A-lice," the echo seemed to call.

Closer my side my friend did press,
In half-way fear and shy alarm;
I felt her heart beat on my arm.

I knew she wondered why each sound
Of voice or step or creaking floor,
Should echo "Alice," nothing more,

Through room and hall and winding tower,
And so I nothing said, while she
Drew close and closer unto me.

With silent voice and noiseless tread,
We reached the mouldy turret stair,
When, breaking shrilly through the air,

The horrid screech of frightened owl
Brought echoes loud from every wall,
Of cellar, attic, tower, and hall.

"Alice," the echoes singly came,
And met and mingled in one note.
So dreadful as they rudely smote

Ceiling and rafter with the sound,
Repeating ever, till they died
Like strangling ghosts on every side.

I felt the heart-beats plainer still,
And tremors with them soon began
To grow electric, as they ran.

We touched the crumbling, mossy stair;
With shadows dark we moved along,
As portion of the spirit throng,

And gained at length a turret small,
Reaching above the palm trees high,
With opening toward the starry sky,

From which the moon, now rising, shone
Down on the forest and the sea,
Down on my gentle maid and me.

"What," said she softly, "can it mean,
This plaintive, changeless echo voice,
Without a varying note of choice?"

"'Tis not an echo, but a call,
A startling, dismal monotone
That might have echoes of its own."

And so I told her, as we sat
Up in that ancient, moonlit bower,
The story of the mouldy tower.

How in the years of long ago
A youthful lover, good and true,
Had planned the castle through and through,

And built it then accordingly
For her he loved more than his life;
For her who was to be his wife.

Sweet Alice Hope, the fairest maid
That ever lived where palm trees grow,
And orange blossoms bud and blow.

And when the castle ready grew,
With shady lawn and garden plot.
With not a beauteous thing forgot,

Or not a thing the heart could wish,
The lover brought his smiling bride
Up to the mansion, by his side.

And there they passed a happy day,
Till night spread o'er the castle high,
Its mantle dark and shrouded sky;

Then, as the lover lay asleep,
Thinking in dreams of his fair bride,
Dark forms did through the castle glide,

While echoes low called out in vain—
From muffled footsteps as they fell—
"It is not well, it is not well."

At midnight hour the lover woke,
And, listening, heard fall everywhere
Faint echoes through the heavy air;

And, starting, found himself alone;
Alone in couch and room and hall;
Alone within his castle wall.

"Alice," he called, "Alice, my love,"
But back into his lonely room
"Alice," came echoing through the gloom.

Then quick the lover rose in fear,
And trembling ran, and wildly cried,
As voice notes into echoes died.

Though weeks went by he never found
Her whom he searched both day and night,
With beating heart and tearful sight,

Till sad he grew, morose and gray.
Till strangely in his eyes there came
The red lamps of unreason's flame;

And through the castle, wild he ran
In maddened frenzy, knowing not
Entreating word or sober thought.

So thus he searched, but never found,
And died at length within the tower
Where sit we at this very hour.

And ever since his maniac voice
Broke jangling discord in the air,
"Alice," is echoed everywhere.

———o———

TO MY NAMESAKE.

FORTUNE and fame are mine, strange chance,
I own!
Deserving neither, I may claim
Both honors in thy infant name!

"Obscure, unknown," I cried, "Ah me!"
And dreamed,
But never that my name would be
Passed downward to posterity!

Yet so it fell about. One night
A soul,
Whose, none can tell, came down to earth
Wrapped in the circle of its girth.

Down from mysterious heights it drew
To us,
When, by some subtle power, unknown,
It snapped apart the virgin zone,

And turned from life of chrysalid
To what,
Though small, is still another I,
Which must into expansion fly,

And see and feel and think and speak
Like men;
Be just as much what others are
As star is like another star.

Well, thanks to kindness, thou dost bear
My name;
Not for the name's sake, but for mine,
And for the sake of auld lang syne.

Though when my head is white, wilt thou
Be young.
When I descend the hill—thy feet
Will reach new paths with footsteps fleet.

Youth will thy guardian be—mine, age.
And so,
When in my ear no voices call,
Thy name will into circles fall.

Some blushing maid will say thy name
In love;
Will write it down full oft, and stay
Upon each writing half the day;

Think what a perfect name to have,
Then add,
Shyly enough, though no one sees,
Such words as may her fancy please.

This will be quite reward enough
For me,
If, watching, I can speak a word
That by my namesake shall be heard.

If, speaking from my rugged hill,
I know
That thou shalt listen as I speak :
"Son, look above; Christ's kingdom seek.

"There is no joy on earth but His,
No peace;
Let Him thine own possession be,
And all things else shall come to thee."

——o——

LOVE FIRST.

To C.

Do you remember how, one tranquil night,
When all the shore along where eye could reach
Tall palms cast graceful shadows on the beach,
And spreading oaks hung low with mystic white,
We lay us down on beds of drifted shells,
And listened long to what the ocean tells?
How waves came rolling from the boundless sea,
With thoughts from far away for you and me,
Of life and love and of eternity?

Life then indeed seemed fair and sweet,
Its years, like passers in the street,
Met thoughtless, without time to greet.

Love! how its very semblance shone
And flashed and warmed. Ah! had we known
How soon its ashes would be sown!

Eternity—the sound we heard,
Though not a leaf of thought it stirred.
The sound we knew, but not the word.

'Twas circle wide to us, but less
Than one small ring of tenderness
Which had no arc of bitterness.

All was encompassed by that ring
Of youthful love; its power could fling
Unreason into sentient thing.

You put the pink shell to my ear,
And, pausing, asked me, "Do you hear
These ocean whisperings soft and clear?"

"Love first," was murmured in the shell,
"Without it, death, the end, may well
Come knocking at your mortal cell.

"Love is the essence of the whole;
Love gave to man his living soul,
Guides, leads, directs as ages roll.

"Love is the mould of all your clay,
And, out of chaos, in one day
Draws Psyche from the far away.

"Life hears the call, more quick obeys,
And runs its current through the maze
Of roads and paths and winding ways.

"Aye, love is God; love could alone
Come from its higher, highest throne
With bounteous proffer to atone

"For all the sin that hate has wrought,
For selfish longing bringing naught
But evil actions from the thought.

"And God is love; he sent love here
To aid, to strengthen, and to cheer;
To make himself to us more dear.

"First love thy God, he first loved thee,
Then life will swift within thee be,
And sweeten thy eternity.

"Get love for love, and life for life;
Gladness for sorrow, peace for strife;
Rest after janglings loud and rife.

"Love thou thy neighbor—God obey—
Though yet he hate thee, love alway;
Love turneth even hate away.

"And she who loves thee—love her well,
For such is love—its broken spell
Has in it all the pangs of hell."

Then ceased the voice within the shell,
And I remember, as the moon went down,
Its crescent dipping in the ocean blue,

I asked the meaning of the voice, but you
Were lost in thought, and answered with a frown,
A sentence long of silence, looking down.

TWO CITIES.

HERE shall I rest, upon this grassy knoll,
Where, lying prone so far below, the great
And noisy city stretches into view,
Keeping along the mighty river's edge
Like clinging child unto its mother's side;
Wherein are living men and moving things
That crowd and jostle forth from day to day,
Among the turrets, towers, and spires, which throw
Their heavy shadows on the surging tide.

Fit place to rest, for nearer yet to me
Lies now a city of the dead. Its streets
Run here and there by habitations dark;
By dim mausoleum, with marbled front,
And sculptured tombs of brass and onyx stone;
By monuments whose tall tops, rising, lift
Their heads above the trees, and glisten there.
No voice is heard; the dead speak not to us
Who wear a flimsy, changing garb. But through
The clear air of this mild September day,
The sound of voices falls upon my ear,—
Voices of mourners who have come to lay
Within its prison place, a dear, cold form;
And through the broken sobs, I hear the noise
Of falling earth upon the coffin thrown,
As slowly back the sad procession moves
Down to the lower city whence it came.

Oh! strange, that side by side these cities be,
One near the river's edge, the other high

Above it, on the reaching mountain-top;
One full of living sights and sounds, and fraught
With what concerns these beating hearts of ours;
Labor and waiting, love and hate and joy;
Sin, sorrow, pain and longing; deep desire
For things we may not have: the other, still
And silent, holding but the shapes of men
Who neither wait nor work, nor love nor hate,
But lie as cold and motionless as are
The pulseless stones that mark their resting-place.
Oh! it is strange and wonderful to see
The hastening, anxious throngs of men which pass
Along that city's street, yet stranger far
To stand among the speechless slabs, and know
That thousands rest there dead and dumb, who ne'er
Will speak again betwixt the earth and sky,—
Lord, soldier, martyr, peasant, priest, and sage,
Mother and father, lover, wife and child,—
Past all expression, pain or joy, and safe
In awful rest within the city's walls.

So thus the days go by, and one by one
From out the city of the living, comes
Some weary traveler to his resting stone.
But none goes back. The city of the dead
Will not refuse a home to anyone
Who seeks it there, but he may not return,
Nor speak, nor sigh, nor tell why he remains
So long in exile. While between the two
I sit and muse, as twilight falls on both
These cities of the living and the dead,

How can I tell in which most mystery lies,
Or whether it be best to quietly sleep
Under some humble mound, or battle on
Still longer for a breathing-place with men.

Whether or not it be, I know that I
Must leave the living, some day, for the dead;
Pass from one city to the other, up
Perhaps unto some mountain-top, perhaps
Down in some valley, to my endless rest.
So, as the shadows cluster darkly down
O'er grave-stone, mound, and winding path,
I nearer feel to these mysterious things
Than to the twinkling city far beneath.

Mt. Royal Cemetery, 1882.

——o——

PECCAVI.

"PECCAVI," cried she, as she fell
Down on the pavement of her cell;
"Peccavi," and the piteous sound
Rang through the corridors around.
"Thou God, my guardian, draw a-nigh,
If not, Great Spirit, let me die;
Thou knowest all, and unto thee
I look for aid. Oh, comfort me!"

A Vestal was she once, but now
Her pledge is broken, and her vow.
Down in the awful, dismal tomb

She, living, goes to meet her doom.
Cold from the wall the water rains,
The warm blood curdles in her veins.
"O holy Spirit!" hear her cry,
"Bid light come in or let me die.

"I never let the fires go out
Upon the altars; and about
My duties e'er I faithful was.
I did obey the vestal laws
In all save this: One lonely day
A kind and dear one came my way;
Long had we loved, and, oh! so well,
But, Guardian, need I further tell?

"He pressed me hard, I told him no,
'Twould bring us only pain and woe,
Though by no choice of mine I took
The vows of chastity; one book
Of many virgins held my name,
And marriage now were wrong and shame.
'Depart,' I cried; 'O dear one, go;
Thou wouldst not ask if thou didst know.'

"Alas! he would not turn away,
Alas! I could not tell him nay.
His outstretched arm, his deep blue eyes,
Made beautiful by sad surprise,
O'ercame my longing, loving heart,
And made the fatal tear-drops start.
The hour of weakness came, and I
Gave what my heart could not deny.

"Father of Heaven, was this wrong
In thy great sight, when all along
I loved him more than lip would tell,
More than ascetic vows could quell?
Thou who art just, oh, judge, I pray
In thine own tender, holy way
Of this my sin, not his, my God,
And help me bear thy chastening rod!

"If 'tis thy righteous will that I
Should in this dreadful dungeon die;
If I deserve such punishment,
And none forgive and none relent,
O Jove, my Father, let me feel
Sweet peace within me gently steal;
Comfort my heart in this dark hour,
And guard me from its awful pow'r."

Ne'er came the maiden from her grave;
Gods that she worshipped could not save.
Her lamp burned low; her food was gone;
The light of day came not at dawn;
And as she prayed, One whom we know
Looked on his stricken child below,
And calmed the heavings of her breast,
With peace from His eternal rest.

——o——

RELEASE.

I.

BEHIND the bars, caged in, a birdling sang
A sorrowing, plaintive song;

"Freedom," the words in quavers rang,
"Denied to me is wrong.
How much, how very much I long
To use these idle wings and fly
Into that broad and open sky!

"The world without me lies so fresh and fair,
So wonderfully grand;
Its flowers and trees and fragrant air,
Its stretching miles of land—
A gift to all from God's own hand—
While in my small, small cage I fret
And sing for what I cannot get.

"Why keep me so? Because I have a voice?
Because my notes are clear?
For sing I must—I have no choice;
Though I should glad my jailer's ear,
And make her care to keep me here,
Through every note I breathe a sigh,
And all my song is all a cry."

Now swiftly to the pavement stone
The cage fell down; its bird had flown;
And, soaring toward the heavenly blue,
It sang a carol as it flew,
Nor saw not on the pavement there
Its jailer with her golden hair,
Her trembling lip and tearful eye,
Sob for her pet with piteous cry:
"Oh, darling bird, come back to me
Come, my own little birdie be!"

II.

Within its bars, caged in, a sad soul lay,
Crying a rending song,
Bearing its pain from day to day,
Through months and years along,
Yet never noticed by a throng
Of dearest friends to sob or sigh,
But softly sing as days went by.

Tho' to One ear the song seemed full of pain,
A symphony of grief—
Sweet, calm, and low in every strain,
Yet asking, praying for relief
Of Him who makes life long or brief,
With words and tears: "O Father, God,
No longer chasten with thy rod.

"Beyond me lies that wondrous, wide expanse,
So great, so far, so high;
For it my bosom throbs and pants,
I would within its pastures lie—
Oh, let me thither, thither fly!
Saviour, I would but view thy face
And leave this narrow, prison place."

Now from two bright eyes, just at eve,
The light went out. Two hands did leave
Their tasks, and fall so cold and still—
Dead servants to an absent will.
Up into Heaven, past heavenly blue,
The spirit gladly, quickly flew,
Nor heard there, bending o'er her clay,

An agonizing husband pray:
" Oh, darling, do not, do not go!—
Without thee all of life is woe."

—o—

GOD RULES.

LET the earth roll
And turn upon its axis round and round;
Swing through the awful sea of space,
Where neither height, nor breadth, nor depth is found;
God rules, above, around!

Darken the sky,
From north to south in banks of blackness, send
Live, livid, flashing tongues of lightning out;
Crash peals of thunder on from end to end;
God rules and will defend!

Toss up the sea,
Into a hundred horrid heavings dark,
Which groan back to uncaverned depths beneath,
Yet from above, beyond, far heavens arc,
God rules and guides the bark!

Let anger rise
Within the heart of man, and words of gall
Burn out their way between his whitened lips;
Let friends betray, or whatsoe'er befall,
God rules, and loveth all.

MNEMOSYNE.

STRETCHING myself upon a bed
 Of beaten sand and withered moss,
I lay full length and watched the red
 Sun send its rays the waves across.

A charm I held within my palm,
 And clasped it tightly, as a dream
With various fancies, fair and calm,
 Did soon my wandering thoughts redeem.

More weary grew I, till there came
 Entrancing rhapsodies of sleep,
To whisper sweet things in the name
 Of her whose love was mine to keep.

"Come," said fair Iris, "take my hand;
 I know thy great desire must be
To view some islets in the Land
 Unbounded by a boundless sea.

"I know thy haunts, and everyone
 Has seen my arch prismatic glow,
When, at the rising of the sun,
 Light fell upon the mists below;

"Or when the moon rose, pale and fair,
 Up from her mystic hiding-place,
And gave the rain-drops in the air
 The color of her cheerful face.

"Be hopeful thou, and follow me;
 If thou wilt but my wish fulfill,

Sweet Memory's handmaid into thee
  Shall all her wealth of charm instill.

"I heard thy wishes, and thy maid,
  Oft have I seen her as she lay,
Her locks disheveled, not afraid
  To let my moon-beams round her play,

"Disclosing beauty that would fill
  Thy soul with trembling, strange delight,
And give thee thoughts to throb and thrill
  Thy pulses swift from morn till night.

"Come thro' this vale of twenty years,
  Grown up with weeds and bramble vine,
And view the scene which now appears;
  Note every shade and every line.

"There, on a grassy slope, and near
  A row of nonage cherry trees,
Some childish forms are seen; they rear
  A hamlet fit for chickadees.

"With anxious look they scheme and plan,
  To make their home the very best;
A house they call it, and again
  Add something to the growing nest.

"'Tis made of broken bough and limb,
  With blossoms hanging down between,
Through which the sunlight pierces dim,
  Resisted by a roof of green.

"Scan well their faces—his and hers;
  List to their laughing, happy play;

See how he bids—how she demurs,
  But how he always has his way.

"Their task is done, and so they sit,
  And talk in quite a serious way;
Speak often with a wholesome wit,
  Not found in those whose heads are gray.

"Thou'rt looking at her auburn hair,
  And at her dark and lustrous eyes,
Low saying—'she, so sweet and fair'—
  I know it well: thy look belies.

"But follow me another way
  Into this woody, winding path,
Where scarce the light of brightest day
  Can touch the lusty aftermath.

"Rememberest thou the pretty walk,
  The grand old trees which met above,
Whose leafy branches seemed to talk,
  And sometimes whisper, of their love;

"And where, beneath a rugged tree,
  Of many limbs and fruitful yield,
Upon the soft grass—list to me,
  Thou hast in earnest tones appealed

"Once on a time—thou but a youth,
  And she more tender far in years,
To whom thou saidst enough, in truth,
  To bring the blushes and the tears?

"Ah! now I see upon thy cheek
  The shadow of her burning blush.

It must be so; thou dost not speak,
  But whisperest strangely, 'Hush thee, hush.'

"So be it then, and now farewell,
  Though thou hast seen but half my span,
Its farther limit reaches well
  Beyond the ken of any man."

* * * * * * *

I starting woke, and found the sun
  Had sunk behind a darkened sea;
The wind blew cold; a fog begun
  To cast its dampness over me.

Out of my mind the fancies went,
  Quick from my hand the trinket fell,
And as my homeward steps I bent,
  I thought of things I cannot tell.

———o———

THE DYING YEAR.

IN the wide hearth the fire burned bright,
And cast about a shadowy light,
    Fitful but cheery;
While close beside an old man sat
And watched the figures on the mat,
    Until a-weary.

His locks were gray, and fell about
Shoulders now bent which once were stout,
    And all his beard

Scrambled along his sunken chest,
And fell upon his faded vest,
In manner weird.

"I am an old man," and his breath
Had in it quavering notes of death,
Trembling, unsteady;
Yet spake he on: "My end draws near,
I see it in the embers here,
But I am ready.

"At midnight hour my knell shall come,
And life within be stricken dumb.
Hark! now I hear
The voice of him who, calling, speaks
In my deaf ear, and cries and shrieks,
'Lo! I am here.

"'I am the new prince, get thee hence,
Thou wrinkled, old Experience,
Go to thy lot;
For I am king, if thou be seer,
And I will rule through all my year
In act and thought.'

"I see down in the embers red
Pictures of scenes that now are fled,
Of days when I was young,
And sang so merrily, and laughed
As from my bowl I gaily quaffed
The wine by muses sung.

"Much have I done for all of you,
Much heard of sayings false and true,

And oft, as well,
Brought life and death into one ring,
A theft and then an offering,
For so the embers tell.

"Rejoicings have I seen, and mirth
Attend the advent of a birth,
With laughing smile;
Then, ere the joy had spent its breath,
I saw the bloodless face of death
And funeral pile.

"So shall it be when this new king
Is old as I, and everything
Leads on to swift decay;
When locks are white, and voice is low;
When life is but an empty show,
And youth has flown away."

Now faint and fainter grew the light;
The embers darkened into night;
No shadows fell;
Till, suddenly, a dying spark
Shot up the chimney, thro' the dark,
While peal of bell

Cried out its notes at midnight hour,
Down from the turret of the tower,
Far, and around,
Pealing in joy, "Our prince is here;"
Tolling in grief, "Farewell, old year,"
One echoing sound.

December, 1887–88.

A MOTHER'S LOVE

[A few months ago an execution took place in the town of S., where I was staying. The unfortunate man was a person about thirty years old, his only living relative being his mother, then seventy years of age. After the sentence of death had been passed, the old woman seemed almost heart-broken, yet she prayed and entreated for pardon. She obtained a number of names to her requisition—it was pitiful to see with what an eager joy she received each signature--and sent her petition to the Governor. After this the mother returned home some hundred miles distant, without a doubt as to the success of her effort. But the fatal day came with no pardon, and the widow's unfortunate boy atoned for his dreadful crime. She came with bending, tottering form alone, and returned alone, sacredly guarding her precious charge with all the love of a mother's immaculate devotion.]

NOT a sad brow in all the throng,
No mellowed voice, but cruel jeers,
There were to take the place of tears;
Death must requite the felon's wrong.

Ah! these are brutes, not men, who stand
To wait and watch in jest and fun,
The trembling steps, the shame of one
Who now gives what his sins demand.

What still? can man give more than all,
Will life and breath not yet atone,
Could not the murderer die alone
And leave the wormwood and the gall?

No; he must take the bitter cup,
Stand and be firm before that gaze;
He faltering stands, but see! he prays
For strength to drink the poison up!

And now the hangman's work is done,
His pulseless victim lies—all white,
His eyelids quivering in the light,
His fingers purpling in the sun.

No pity! not a one to sigh!
Does no heart sorrow o'er this pall,
This retribution of a fall?
Is it then nothing thus to die?

Yes, one alone weeps; hear her cry,
Full, full of anguish and of woe.
Has ever woman suffered so,
Since God of mercy ruled on high?

Alone the feeble mother stands
Beside the body of her boy,
He who was once her love and joy,
To close his eyes and fold his hands.

Her head bends low, the tears fall fast,
Her wrinkled hands clasp his again,
And in the anguish of her pain
She falls insensible at last.

Poor mother, now thy boy is dead,
His guardian must thou be in death,
As when he drew his infant breath,
And from thy willing bounty fed.

And that which kept him in his youth,
And sang him often into sleep;
That often did his vigils keep,
Was love which must prevail, like truth.

No common love can such love be,
For with it can no love compare;
It is than precious jems more rare,
And yet 'tis boundless as the sea.

A mother's love—who has not known
The beauty of its holy light,
That shines alike by day or night,
With gaining strength though older grown.

San Francisco, February, 1885.

——o——

PSYCHE.

I.

WHAT soul is this that has come down to our earth to-day,
Perfect, immortal, unchanging, changeless forever?
How came it thence and thus from its home so far away,
Where beginning ne'er was and ending is never?

Why, coming down, must it serve and obey like a slave,
Be what a casket, perishing, imperfect, would make it?
Tossing 'twixt fear and pain; pressed like the wave
When the wind and the storm in fury o'ertake it.

Taken from high estates unto a low one; held
Prisoner within the dank walls of dust, earth, and clay;

Wonder 'tis not our spirits have cried, have rebelled,
Have shouted and shrieked for some light of the hidden day.

Buried and dungeoned in cavern and cave, in the dark,
Indiscerptible souls are in this discerptible dust;
An essence of purity, goodness, and truth—near the stark
Naked forms, shameless postures of lies, hate and lust.

Idiots, insane, sick, the deformed, helpless and maimed,
Given for slave what is higher than angels in Heaven;
Used and reused for things that can never be named;
Used and reused for the devil seven days out of seven.

II.

To the soul belong joy, faith, peace, goodness, and love,
Temperance, meekness and charity, deep hatred of strife,
For coming from Him, it is His, and like Him above
Why should it, why should it be, a part of such life?

III.

In the arm, and the hand, and the eye, and the ear, and the tongue,
Sin lives, and flows thro' the veins, and quivers the nerves along,
Though it shine and glitter like the stones it was written there hung
In some goblin's cave, it is crime—it is shame—it is wrong.

For the works of the flesh are hatred, revenge, and ill,
Idolatry, selfishness, revilings, and envy and wrath,
Emulations, drunkenness, seditions, a murderous will;
These are the thorns of flesh, these are the thorns the soul hath.

IV.

And the only joy of the soul is the day of our death,
When this burden of clay shall fall; when the soul may fly
On the wings of a never-returning breath,
To its home, where is nothing that maketh a lie.

—o—

SILENCE.

To Dr. S.

Ah, yes! silence is eloquent, and tells
To you and me of things we cannot say
In the poor language of this shallow world.
As when the day of parting comes, and I
Clasp all your hand in mine, and, in your eye,
Look to the deepening depths of your great soul,
Seeing there more than all our pens could write
On all the paper made, or to be made.

As when the lover gazeth upon her
Who rests her head upon his throbbing heart,
And gazeth silently, yet speaketh not.

Silence is language of the soul, and speaks
Ne'er so a third can hear, nor does it sound
Through air, or to the ear of any man.
It comes as light comes to the mountain-top,
Or as those shadows, falling on its side,
Is, yet is not, like space which holds our worlds;
Is nothing of itself, and has no form,
No bulk, no magnitude, nor anything.

When, after all the peals of music deep,
Which issued from the organ loft, there comes
An end, you still can hear, so low and sweet,
Within your soul the same notes o'er again,
With variation added, and you know
That silence is the mother of the strain.

In the great aisle of some cathedral dark,
When night has come and not a soul is near,
Listen you well to silence, which shall speak
Unto your heart as never spake there man.
Or, move out to the graves that lie as still
As children sleeping when the day has fled.
Sit down awhile and catch the thrill that runs,
Like some electric current, to your soul,
Bringing you thought on thought, until your mind
Flows over, and you break the magic spell,
By breaking silence in some uttered word.

What made the harps that weary wanderers hung
Up, on the willows, in the olden time
By Babylonian rivers, yet convey
More thrilling notes, and deeper music far
Than when their many strings were fingered o'er
And strung? Or why should all the world, and you,
Not hear Tiara's harp till silence struck
Her trembling fingers on its every cord?
Who cannot shake the air with words and words
And cast them in your ear? But gods have oft
Not able been to even guard their lips
From speaking into death their dearest hope
And wish. So thus the brooklet babbles on,

And tells a shallow tale to every man,
While on the noble river deepening flows,
And silent is. No man shall know how deep
The river runs, until he come and see.

And now thought to the outward ear speaks not,
Though thought is father of the universe,—
Sea, air, sky, rocks, and earth but children are
Of this great silent Thought that speaks to you
Alone, or me alone, but never speaks
So you and I can learn at once the word.
And what are words to thought? As moon to sun,
Night unto day, and hate to loving are.
Silence is like to faith, and words to works.
Both words and works but hint the wondrous power
Of faith and silence, for it hath been told
That silence is the language of the gods.

—o—

THE CLOCK AND THE OWL.

On two shelves in his office a banker once kept,
Cheek by jowl,
A clock and an owl.
The former for use and the latter for show,
A hollow pretence one, of feathers, you know;
An owl stuffed with sawdust, but looking as well
As though it were sleeping at noon in the dell.
Just as wise as a being can possibly look,
Who never wears glasses nor reads from a book.

But one night very late, when the bank lights were out,

The owl called the clock a pestiferous lout,
A thing quite uncalled for, especially when
Polite to its partner the time-piece had been.
"Oh, when will you cease," sneered the owl with a mock,
"With your endless twaddle and tiresome talk;
Cease holding the minutes of every hour
Like some old gauge holds the drops of a shower.
What good is it all, I would like to know,
To measure out minutes just so and so?
You stand on the shelf and all through the night
Your pendulum sways from left hand to right,
And your hands are held up to your sallow face,
Like a child that has fallen into disgrace.
Not often one deigns to hear what you say,
Tho' sometimes 'tis done in a casual way;
But often I see, and oft have I heard,
That no one has taken or trusted your word.
As you point to the hour and strike it again,
They will look at their watches, both women and men."

"Sneer and talk all you will,
I shall tick on still,
Though you snap out more wrath from your crooked bill.
I am doing my duty, while you, ugly owl,
Have nothing to do but to grumble and growl,
And all through the day
Not a word will you say,
But make people think, with your large, open eyes,
You are learned and knowing and wondrously wise.

"I am plain, I confess it, my hands both are coarse,

And my voice very often is husky and hoarse.
Then, fearing my memory, I tick through the night,
So the hours of the day be kept proper and right,
For I never go wrong—you may ask whom you will,
And this is the reason I never keep still.

"The busy consult me; the idle I warn
By showing how quickly the eve follows morn,
By counting each moment of time as it goes,
By telling it over, when everyone knows.
If I ticked only hours, the world would go by
Like a ship on the sea or a cloud in the sky,
And life would escape without thought or endeavor,
And minutes and seconds be lost us forever.
But now every second I call men to work,
With all of twice sixty less chances to shirk.
'Come, come,' so I call, and they haste to obey;
'Come, come,' every second I solemnly say,
Though totals deceive us, the details will tell
Us fairly our standing, you know very well.
Our fortunes by dollars may quickly be told,
But by mills and by dimes will they greatly unfold.

"You sneer at my duties and think they are small,
Because you are idle, and have none at all,
But, sphinx-like, you stand on your pedestal shelf,
Puffed up and all ruffled with glorious self.
You are laid on the shelf in more senses than one;
If you ever were useful, your mission is done.

"When the banker comes down in the morning, he looks
At my face just a second, then takes out his books,
For at seven precisely my orders I get,

And never one order I shirk or forget.
If you think I am useless keep awake for one day,
And see how they watch me and hear what I say.
At six one consults me and sweeps off the floor;
At ten one consults me, then opens each door;
So they quiz me and ask me 'what hour,' all the day,
And the answer I give them they never gainsay."

"Oh! you are for labor," the sage owl replied,
And puffed up his feathers in anger and pride;
"No gentleman, truly, I have at my side.
I knew by your talk you belonged to the rabble.
I pity you now—but continue your babble;
Pay no notice to me, yes, talk when I talk,
You miserable, garrulous, plebian clock.
Though they quiz you and hear you, oh! do not believe
Their questions you answer or their minds you relieve,
For each question they ask you, they give me a wink,
As much as to say, 'Now what do you think,
He's a babbling old fool and he never keeps still,
But let him go on while there's gold in the till;
You are Capital, friend, that fellow is Labor,
We are catering now for his vote, O my neighbor.'

"So what are you here beside me, little clock,
Though you think you are much, and chatter and talk?
They respect me and fear me, but you they can use;
If me they neglect, you they often abuse;
In this bank I for money, you for labor do stand,
I for dollars and cents, you for muscle and hand.

But I'll lose no more wit on you ticking old thing,
I am tempted to push you plumb off with my wing,
I can do it so quickly and well if I like—
There! you're wheezing and rattling and off on a strike."

"I would rather *be* something than stand for a billion;
You are poor, boastful owl, though your master has
million.
What are being and doing to having, I wonder,
As fire is to smoke, or as lightning to thunder!
'Time is money,' we say, yet you scorn time and labor;
Beware of your sawdust and feathers, O neighbor!"

"More room do I want," said the banker one day;
"I must move this old owl or our timepiece away,
The owl we can spare, but we cannot the clock."
So they took down the owl with its shelf and its block,
And put them away in the vault with the money,
Up high in the corner, oh! wasn't it funny?

——o——

THE THRONG.

IN a strange city,
With no one to greet you,
No one to love,
Though many to meet you,
Hurrying and rushing, the crowd moves along,
An anxious, a busy, a marvelous throng.

No one to look down
In sympathy cheering,

No one to give
  You a word of endearing,
Though you be starving to love and be cherished,
Seem heart and love among men to have perished.

See there a sweet face,
  With eyes soft and tender!
Will not his crying
  For pity unbend her?
Ah, no! she casts but a glance at his tatters,
Then turns away to less troublesome matters.

What is a beggar
  Here, crying for pity?
Hundreds are standing
All over the city,
Yet hurrying, rushing, the crowd moves along,
A selfish, a cruel, a passionless throng.

Suicides, murders,
  Oh, terrible trifling,
How can I stay here,
  The air is so stifling!
Come away, soul, from these scenes of disaster,
Come to the mountain and rest, like the Master.

San Francisco, Cal., November, 1885.

——o——

MY CHOICE.

WITHIN her soft, pink hand
  She held a lily, pure and white.

Its pistils trembled at her heart's
Each joyous pulse-beat, quick and light.
Like babe asleep it lay so still,
Breathing, yet without breath or will.

She held it up to me,
The lily in her lily hand,
And of the two full well I knew
Which would my praises best demand.
I looked upon them both, and thought
Ne'er fairer workmanship was wrought.

One liveth not—but one
Is pink and warm, and can obey
The dictates of a higher will,
Though be it, like the flow'r, of clay;
Much can it grant, and much express
Of love, or aid, or willingness.

"*I'll take the gem away,*"
Now spoke a voice reproachfully;
"I cannot hold it here for you
To simply gaze upon, nor say
What beauty has it in your eye,
So then, indifferent man, good-bye."

"Stay, my fair friend," I cried,
"Thought took all power of speech away,
I saw what was so beautiful,
More came to me than I could say;
I know the flower may pretty be,
But lovelier far the hand to me.

"For seeing both, I thought
How much the hand more than the flower
Seems beautiful. Knowing how great,
In deeds of kindness, is its power;
How thro' it all the current red
Flows from the heart and from the head."

The maid's cheek crimson grew,
She did not mean her hand, she said,
But what lay in its hollowed palm;
Then tossed aloft her haughty head:
"I meant the lily, not the hand;
How hard for men to understand!"

But obstinate I stood,
I would not understand at all,
Until the hand I firmly held—
Her hand, so warm and soft and small,
Nor did I let it go till she
Had given it away to me.

——o——

SINCERITY.

If you think so, say so,
Do;
I would rather 'twere said,
If true.
'Tis better to take the rough thorn out,
Than to fret and whine and cry about
The pain which it gives to you.

If 'tis a thought you hate,
Now, pray,
Treat it with scorn and scowl;
For we may
Sometimes have thoughts that we do not love,
Which come from below, and not above,—
From night-time and not from day.

They are but crows that fly
Along
Into our pure, white air.
Soon a song-
Bird may follow and sweetly sing,
And, dove-like, pass over the croaking thing,
As Right flies over Wrong.

Blame you I never would—
No,
Not for a strayward thought,
For I know
There are thoughts that wander about for homes;
They are stalking shadows of ugly gnomes,
Which travel to and fro.

Bony and gaunt and thin,
Dead
To loving and peace and joy;
They are wed
By angry ghosts to the sprites of hell,
And their breed, how monstrous, I cannot tell,
By monsters bred.

True thoughts are like the rain,
Fresh,
Down from the clouds of heav'n.
Poor flesh
And blood have not many to spare—
Some, sometimes, there are, but rare, rare, rare,
And mixed in a mixed-up mesh.

——o——

JEALOUSY.

Of all the wicked sins that keep
Down in the sinful heart of man,
Of all the monsters of the deep,
Of all the horrid things that creep
In Ashantee or Hindostan,
None are so falsely, fiercely wild
As this Briareus-handed child,
This jealous wrath that sets the heart on fire,
And rakes the burning coals of base desire.

Truly 'tis said to be the sin
Of an ignoble, selfish mind,
That seeks no gentler grace to win,
But gladly lets the baser in
So it possessorship may find,

While wholesome word and action die,
And all the holier promptings fly.
Thus jealous anger does its direful work
And stabs brave manhood with a subtile dirk.

Look through the records of the past,
Down through the history dark of Rome;
Think but a moment of the vast
Recorded crimes, like raging blast
That sweep before its Arching Dome!
To jealous spirit trace may we
Their murder, hate, and tyranny,
In ancient king or haughty autocrat,
'Neath jeweled crown or laboring peasant's hat.

Through England's line of rulers vain,
Through all the deadly throes of France,
Through centuries that wax and wane
In sad degrees of strife and pain,
Through secret stab or open lance,
We see the shape of that dark face
Grin from its gloomy, dismal place,
Cast deep its lurid, burning gaze, and bring
All other shades to its own coloring.

When Juno jealous grew, she wrought
With other gods her jealous spite;
How to revenge she planned and thought,
Evil continually she brought—
Nor ever after knew delight,
But, dwelling with the selfish elf,
Grew into bitterness itself.

So anciently, when one had sinned, they sent
Waters of jealousy for punishment.

'Twas this that filled the heart of Cain
With hate instead of tender love;
That gave fire to his maddened brain;
That bade him call aloud in vain
To God for blessings from above,
Till, ruled by jealousy, he killed
His brother Abel—basely spilled
The life-blood of his kinsman to the ground,
And gained a heavy burden for the wound.

Busiris righteous was beside
A jealous spirit in the heart;
For only evil 'twill betide,
Nor with it e'er can good abide;
It bids kind Charity depart,
And, like the tyrant, it will feed
Pure, tender feelings to its greed.
O man, beware, let not the tempter nigh;
Pray God he keep thee from its evil eye!

——o——

A CAROL.

THE first sweet Christmas, when a Saviour's birth
  Came, like the light of dawn, from heav'n above,
Bringing good-will to men and peace to earth,
  With blessed tidings of a Father's love,

Wise men from far came to the lowly bed
On which the King of Peace, uncrowned, lay;
Gave treasures rich, then, with uncovered head,
In rev'rence bow'd, and gave their hearts away.

And as night, dark'ning o'er the wide plains, fell,
Touch'd every sloping foot-hill far and near,
While all was still, save when some tinkling bell
Rang its clear notes upon the shepherd's ear,

Light flash'd in darkness; and a rushing sound
Of many voices, full and rich and strong,
Shook all the waves of air, fell to the ground,
And through the plains and valleys rolled along.

"Fear not," the angels sang, "for there is born
Unto you all this day a Saviour King,
As to the darkness is the rising morn,
So unto you is He; arise and sing."

Then all the shepherds sang with mighty voice,
"A Saviour unto us is born, rejoice! rejoice!"
And yet the music floated down again,
"Yea, peace for earth is and good-will to men,
Rejoice, a Lord is born, rejoice, rejoice."

Yule Tide, 1886.

——o——

THE WAY OF THE WORLD.

Up and down,
High and low,
Broad and narrow,
Fast and slow,

Plough and harrow,
Fade and blow.
Life and death,
First and last,
Beginning and end,
Present and past,
So they blend
And contrast.
Coming and going,
Reaping and sowing,
Laughing and crying
Living and dying;
All in one day,
Here, and away.
Shifting and shifting,
Drifting and drifting,
Onward we go;
In changes, forever,
We meet and we sever,
For gladness or woe.

——o——

TO A YOUNG FRIEND.

THE diamond is not found encas'd with gold,
Nor are pearls hidden in a showy case;
Fortunes, we know, are buried in the mould,
And truths upheld in many an untow'rd place.

Look, then, within; yes, far within
The outer mouldings of this clay,
There lives what will affection win,
The soul it is—the heart, we say.

'Tis hidden deep, perhaps, but thou
  Mays't polish off the rough without;
Thy small, soft fingers well know how
  To bring the much desired about.

——o——

EVENA.

"θεῆς εἰς ὦπα ἔοικεν."

THEY do not flash, her eyes,
  But they sparkle and shine,
Reflecting the kindly light
  Of a soul divine;
I wish—I have often wished—
  Their dark orbs were mine.

Mine to look into—and
  Mine, to have love express,
With, oh! such a wealth and power
  Of deep tenderness;
With virtue to cheer, I know,
  And comfort and bless.

Better than words they speak
  Out what the heart would say,
Bidding me wait and hope
  Till another day—
When clouds which threaten low
  Have all cleared away.

——o——

PROVIDENCE.

WE sow the seed, and we may reap
  The harvest flower,

LIBRARY
OF THE
UNIVERSITY
OF
CALIFORNIA.

IN OUR LAND

But God alone can watch and keep;
Lo! when our eyelids droop in sleep
He sends the shower.

——o——

IN OUR LAND.

BRIGHT days have we in our land so fair,
No frost ever breathes through the balmy air,
Snow and ice we chain to their mountain lair,
And sunshine is radiant everywhere.
And the skies are blue all over the land,
Over valley and hill;
Beautiful blossoms on every hand
Open their treasures at our demand,
And the wafted air
Is freighted with odors sweet and rare,
Of laurel, acacia, jessamine,
Myrtle, marjoram, wild eglantine,
Lily and orange and lavender.

——o——

CHRISTMAS-TIDE.

(TO JAMIE.)

AGAIN the sea of time reaches our shore
With its full tide of joy and cheer,
Bearing up to us ships of tokens—more
The lasting trophies of a Christmas year.

And as, when waves roll back, there lie
  Shells, mosses, stones, and coral rare,
For some to take, and by and by
  Keep as mementoes sweet and fair,

So the full wave of Christmas-tide
  Bears down upon us all to-day,
Bringing dear tokens to our side
  For us to take and lay away,

To treasure in our hearts their worth,
  Not for themselves but what they show,
Love for each other—what on earth
  Greater or better could we know?

It is not then for treasure rich
  We ask now at this happy time,
But only words of sweet assurance, which
  Are tokens of a love sublime,

Sublime because 'tis true and deep;
  Precious because 'tis pure,
Oh! such a love will surely keep
  Our hearts and minds secure!

If the great sea would try to bring
  A fitting token of its might,
The grandeur of its offering
  Would startle—not delight.

Mine then a token is, but small,
  For our great love cannot a token find;
To search one out would only pall,
  And turn expression blind.

The sun sends down a joyful gleam,
  Why not be happy as the birds;
The skies are beautiful, and seem
  To speak for us the words:

"Good-will and peace to everyone,
  Now not a single cloud have we
To mar the brightness of our sun—
  Come, let your loving hearts be free."

A merry Christmas then on this fair day,
  And merrrier ones through coming years;
May gladsome cheer chase care away
  And leave behind no place for tears.

And with this wish I pray that He
  Who gave us what we have to give,
May fill our hearts with love—so we
  Shall praise His goodness while we live.

December 25, 1886.

——o——

SUNNYSIDE.

In dreams, both day and night, oft do I go
Back to thy paths, sweet Sunnyside, and see
Thy dear old haunts so fraught with memory
Of all now loved and sacred here below;
View thy fair form and hear the soft winds blow
Down through the bow'rs where, oh! so often, we
As children played in loving harmony,
Brother and sister, nor did even know
The precious value of the passing joy

That filled the hours which went from morn till eve,
And thinking less of cares that might annoy,
Or throbbing pain which tears may not relieve,
For weary thoughts could not our minds employ,
Till added years had taught our hearts to grieve.

——o——

FEAR NOT.

Do not borrow
From to-morrow
  Grief and pain;
With the present
Though unpleasant
  Cope again!

Storms may thunder,
And, far under,
  Waters roll;
Still abiding,
God is guiding
  Safe the soul!

——o——

LOOK UP.

All worldly glory is but vain,
  Though charm it may the youthful heart.
Look up! if thou would'st e'er attain
  True honor and a worthy part

Seek higher things, the kingdom of our God,
And trust his holy will alway;
Follow in love the humble path he trod,
Which leads unto the everlasting Day.

—o—

TO A CHILD.

DEAR child, so pure,
I pray that ne'er
The shadow of thy father's sin
Shall fall upon thy soul within!

He was not true,
And holy love
Touched not his heart with sacred fire;
His was the love of base desire,

Which, satisfied,
Kindled anew,
And left a broken-hearted maid
To bear the burdens he had laid.

He did not know,
Nor aught cared he,
Whether thine eyes would ever view
Earth's beauty or the skies of blue,

But wandered far
In distant lands,
Thoughtless of one to whom he gave
The wound that brought her to the grave.

She did not die
With friends around
To comfort in the trying hour,
But died without a friend or flower,

One single flower
To cheer her way,
As through the awful vale of death
She went with faltering step and breath.

And when she lay
So dead and cold,
No gentle hand did kindly care
To smooth her locks of wavy hair,

But youth and age,
Maiden and sire,
Cast from their minds all thought of her
Whose only sin had been to err

In loving much
The heart of one
Whose hellish deed, I pray, may meet
Reward at God's own Judgment-seat!

Yet—I am wrong,
Dear child, I know,
To rake these ashes of the past
And into present fair winds cast

Their blinding dust;
Without my prayer
A Nemesis will surely come
And strike the evil-doer dumb.

My hope is then,
Sweet child, for thee;
God grant thee manhood pure and strong,
To bear the right and fight the wrong.

——o——

RECONCILIATION.

My heart was tender, so I cried,
"Speak out, O heart! through quivering lip;
Speak now before the moments slip;
Speak softly, gently, near her side,
And tell her 'twas in anger spoke,
The soul doth ask forgiveness now;
Yea, haste ere thought all utterance choke,
Or on her young, untroubled brow
The marks of sorrow deeply plough."

And thus within my heart replied:
"I cannot beg forgiveness yet,
But could she come and ask me why
I said those words, I would reply,
And press these trembling lips to hers.
Confess my sin with tearful eye,
And earn forgiveness by and by.
I cannot ask, but, oh! I pray
God grant me it this very day."

And as she wept, while scalding tears
Rolled down upon her feverish cheek,
These cruel lips refused to speak,

Which they had never done for years.
Then cried I out: "Do now with hand
Stretch out to her thy willing aid,
Encircle her as with a band,
That she may never be afraid;
Haste soon and cheer the grieving maid."

Then once again my heart replied:
"These hands are burning now to press
Heart unto heart. Against my own
To keep hers there until have flown
All cause for weeping and for tears.
Her sob is answered by a moan;
Oh! that I kinder words had known;
If she could lift one pleading hand
Mine both would answer her demand."

Implored I now: "Turn both those eyes
With loving glance into her own;
Show her that they have kindly grown
As after clouds the summer skies."
And turning such a flood of light,
Of love and soulful longing too,
As well would chase the darkest night
And let the rays of sunshine through,
Two dark eyes gazed into the blue.

And pride gave way to contrite tears,
And hand went out in manly aid,
And lip expressed in loving word
What was received and gladly heard.
In long embrace and pressure warm

Smothered was every trace of pain,
And well I know that winter storm
Can never toss our sea again.

——o——

BY THE CLOCK.

SIXTY seconds by the clock,
Sixty ticks and that is all,
Sixty only: as we talk
Down upon the garden walk
Shadows deep begin to fall.
Sixty minutes by the clock,
Made of pulse-beats quick and small,
But a dear soul takes its flight
Up from earth to realms of light,
While hot tears bedim our sight;
Death has come, and that is all.

"Sixty long hours by the clock,
Sixty only, yet alone,
All alone, I sit and rock,
As the seconds laugh and mock
Every sigh and every moan.
Sixty days marked by the clock,
How my face has older grown,
Gray hairs with the brown ones lie;
Wrinkles deep and faded eye,
Plainer grow as days go by,

"Sixty weeks of tearless grief,
Sixty weeks so sad and long,
Asking Heaven for relief,
Praying that my life be brief,
Yet resistless borne along.
Sixty months, the very chief
Of the chiefest, all along
When the heart learns, oh! how deep
Do the chords of sorrow keep,
Though the sounds of sorrow sleep,
Like sad notes of untouched song.

"Sixty years by seconds told,
Minutes, hours, and days as well,
Weeks and months; now I am old,
'Youth is silver, age is gold,'
I will say, since poets tell.
Time in eighty years has rolled,
By clear strokes upon its bell,
All my youth and strength away,
Turned to snowy white the gray,
Breathed cold winter into May,
Warned me I must say farewell."

. . . .

Sixty seconds by the clock,
Sixty seconds, that is all,
Once again the shadows stalk
Through the garden and the walk;
Now they tremble on a pall.
It has come again—the shock
That to each must soon befall.
Though the clock ticks on the sill,

Heart-throbs, pulse-beats now are still,
Throb and beat they never will—
Death has come, and that is all.

———o———

THE EBB AND FLOW.

'Tis an ebb and a flow
Of the ocean wide,
Of the tireless tide.
It is coming and going the long hours through,
Rushing along in its beaten track,
Onward and upward and forward and back,
To its paths in the rocks and the sand,
Here and on every hand.
What it brings it will take away,
What it takes it will give again—
Even as rain clouds give the rain—
Scme day.

If we only knew,
And we all may know,
This life of ours is an ebb and a flow,
Of days and of years,
Of joy and of woe.
And, like the tide that breaks on the rocks
And throws in the air its briny spray,
Is the tide of our life which bears along
Toward the ragged rocks of ill and of wrong,
That cast through our years
Their spray of tears.

By our Tide
Must we all abide;
What it brings it will take away—
What it takes it will give again—
All but the woe and the pain—
Some day.

Laguna Beach, August, 1886.

—o—

YOU.

It is you and no one else
Who have taken my hope and my heart;
You know it not; perhaps if you knew
You would tremble and start.

Now you are thoughtless and young,
And you think not I do not forget;
What you told me once I have kept
And treasured, and hold it yet.

Are words of love nothing, that you
Should sound them in every ear?
Is it as well not to think what you say
As to speak and be sincere?

I would not die if you said
You loved another man better than me;
I would not break in my grief,
But bend, like the willow tree,

Then swing to my place again
After the storm had passed,

For sorrow alone cannot kill a man,
  Though it hold him fast.

But you told me not the truth,
  For you uttered a pack of lies;
And all you said to me was as false
  As the false light in your eyes.

You are the cause of my wandering
  Out from the paths of right;
Pointing, you told me where to go,
  And I went down into night.

Then you kept me in the darkness,
  Though I walked along till I fell
Headlong almost to the very gates
  Of a deep abysmal hell.

"Do this for my love," you said,
  And whatever you asked was done;
I would love all you love, and hate
  Whatever you wished to shun.

Did I do right? Ask your conscience,
  I am not much in doubt;
Blind I was, blinder than Hecuba
  After her eyes were out.

——o——

THE WISER PLAN.

BENEATH an oak a lazy croaker lay
Long after sunrise and the dawn of day,

To fret, to worry, and to whine,
To find some fault with workmanship divine
"Why," said he glibly, "should there be
Pumpkins on vines, and acorns on a tree?
The vines are tender, while the trees are tough;
Acorns are small, but pumpkins large enough.
If God in trees had hung these pumpkins large,
And given to vines the lesser charge,
I'm sure we all could then agree
That it a wiser plan would be."
Just then from its high perch an acorn fell
Into the croaker's face and hit him well,
Which was reproof and argument at once
Sufficient to convince the veriest dunce,
Though, through the mercy of God's wiser plan,
We were not spared the wit of such a man.

——o——

A SONNET.

[To a little blue-eyed lassie who sits near me in church.]

PASSING strange these blue eyes are,
Shining like some merry star
    In the sky!
Only more these two will say,
And in quite a different way,
Than those twinkling from the gray
    By and by!

Eyes that would, yet may not, frown
If they try, can but look down

With a smile;
In whose depths, so sweet and pure,
Sleep expressions which I'm sure
Will some day some heart allure
And beguile!

Hide these eyes with fan or screen,
Snowy white or leafy green,
For a while,
And you find that in a glance,
In a look that will entrance,
Stealing through by merest chance,
Comes the smile!

——o——

THE RAIN.

FAR from the hill-tops there comes a sweet strain,
Louder it echoes now over the plain,
And through the valleys the sound thrills again:
"The rain, the rain."

Down on the hard, on the dry, scorching ground,
Patters the rain with a musical sound,
As from each flower a fair, trembling cup,
Begs of the rain to be quickly filled up.

Oh! was there ever such mirth on the prairie,
Did one e'er see so many so merry?

Trillions of blossoms are gladdening the air,
Sending their fragrance out everywhere,

Tingeing the valley with red and with blue,
Such tints and colors the world never knew!
See! on the mountain the blue bells are ringing,
Larkspurs and poppies and daisies are singing,
And the whole plain is stirred in commotion
Like that which stirs the depth of the ocean.

List! all the flowers ecstatic are crying,
Shouting and dancing, their gay colors flying,
Well may old Chronos now wonder what mirth
Could thus have taken possession of earth.
"Be merry, dear comrades," the trillions flowers sing;
Long live our kind master, and long be he king;
So fill up your cups, be they blue, red, or yellow,
And drink to the health of a jolly good fellow."

Not a bud but was drunk with the rain,
Not a cup but would fill up again,
Not a frond but would join the refrain.

"I thank thee, O Lord! I have not come in vain,"
Sang the rain.

——o——

LINES.

[On seeing the night-blooming cereus open in church on Easter night.]

AND without sun or light, just at the hour
When darkness reigns supreme in ev'ry place,
Slowly unfold, with ever changeless grace,
The waxen petals of a snowy flow'r,

Which, softly stealing from their mystic bow'r,
Ope, all unbidden by that cheerful face
Whose smile and glance become the royal mace
That gives to pregnant buds the magic pow'r.
Like to this flower came One from high above
When all was dark, down to our earth below,
Unfolding one by one His acts divine,
And showing us the beauty of that love
Which our cold hearts ask'd not, yet now may know
And prove the wisdom of God's great design.

——o——

CLOUDS.

TOSSED are the clouds in the sky,
Hurried and pushed by the wind;
So are the strange doubts that fly
Into my wondering mind.

Shadows do fall from the clouds
Down to the valley below;
As from my doubts, ghostly shrouds
Of sadness forever flow.

They fall o'er a longing life,
Casting a shadow and gloom,
Telling of sorrow and strife,
And giving no sunlight room.

Will these, like clouds in the sky,
Which bring us sweet showers of rain,
Refresh us, and by and by
Send sunshine and warmth again?

6

CARELESS WORDS.

In careless mood I shot a bird
And broke its tender little wing;
It fell from the great tree; I heard
A cry escape the fluttering thing;

And such a plaintive cry it gave,
So full of meaning and of pain,
I would have given all to save
That bird from harm again.

So oft our words, without a thought
Of the deep woe they may convey,
Are careless spoken, to be caught
And hidden in some heart away.

No cry may fall upon our ear,
Of the great sorrow that they bring;
We do not often see the tear
When we ourselves feel not the sting.

But such words missiles are, and keen
To sink into the heart of some dear child,
And there, with cruel power unseen,
Work out their mission, fierce and wild:

For what is the heart but a tender thing,
As easily crushed as a birdling's wing!

——o——

LINES WRITTEN ON THE ILIA OF AN OLD SKELETON.

Come! grinning maiden, let us be
More cheery on this stormy e'en,

Stand by the light, where I can see
  Your socket eyes and visage lean;
Loll not with such a drooping air,
For surely you are free from care
And have no scruples, at this day,
But which should all be cast away!
Play not the prude to-night with one
Who bleached your long bones in the sun.

When soft flesh covered all these bones,
  I heard, and know it very well,
Your name was Mary Ellen Jones,
  And you were quite a lively belle;
You drank a little, to be sure—
Some whisky punches taken pure—
And sometimes in a fight you found
Your nasal beaten hard and sound,
And once or twice you had to bear
The pulling of your flaxen hair.

Chicago was your home: ah, well,
  That may explain your wayward life,
And how, at length, you sadly fell
  Into a constant round of strife.
You broke your radius one night
In a disreputable fight,
Which caused me once to really make—
It looked so odd—a sad mistake:
I thought 'twas natural, and lo!
In my report described it so.

I do not know, but I have heard,
  You worked your jaw-bone swift and sure

In billingsgate and evil word;
  For you were not an epicure.
But though the motion's gone, I see,
This bone once moved most rapidly,
When angry would you snap those teeth
Like sword within its scabbard sheath,
Bend up your phalanges, and swing
Your humerus like some flapping wing.

Oft did your metatarsals err
  And take you where you should not go;
And, from appearance, I infer
  You often stubbed your leading toe.
One clavicle is cleft in twain
And never can be used again,
While all the larger bumps you own
Would phrenologically atone
For many sins that you have done,
My cold and dismal skeleton!

You had a lover once who paid
  You kind attentions for a year,
But, like a cruel, heartless maid,
  You dropped him off without a tear;
Yea, without warning word, or fuss,
Sank all his hope in Erebus.
Ah! do I see you laugh, and hear
Those dry bones rattle in my ear,
Ribs, shafts, phalanges, jaws, and all,
Like wind-blown branches in the fall?

Then I have stirred at last your soul,
  Old maid, so gaunt and tall and thin;

Come, help me quaff my student bowl
  And drink its inspiration in!
For I am weary all alone
Conning these leaves on flesh and bone;
A word or two of present aid
Would help me on, O bony maid!
So clasp my hand, and tell me o'er
Tales from the dark Cerberian shore!

——o——

TO GRIEF.

COME, grief, why need'st thou have a fear?
Know thou art not a stranger here.
My heart and thee in sad embrace
Too oft have shown each other grace,
And parents been to sob and tear.

For we are wedded: grief and I
Shall not be severed till we die,
Though sighs and sobs and sometimes tears
May be our offspring, as the years
Of weary waiting shall go by.

——o——

FRAGMENT.

[Written on the back of an envelope addressed to the author, in Mr. Longfellow's handwriting.]

THINE own dear hand did write
These letters each, and all,

Forming my name upon the white
With rise and fall.
And, as I look, I seem to see
Thee sit beside thy writing board;
Take out, where many more were stored,
A parchment, and to me
Give up a moment that might be
Spent writing, for eternity
Some word of sweetest song.

But no! to me belong
The pen and hand and moment too,
As light thy fair hand glides along,
Then stays to cross the letters through;
Seal envelope and lay it down
Upon thy study desk of brown.
I wonder if thou gavest a thought
To me thou ne'er hadst seen,
Whose name to thee by chance was brought
By written go-between?
And if thou saidst upon thy lip
My name, as it would sound in air,
Lest thou shouldst let a letter slip
Or seem to want a care?

I do not know; but this I know,—
I love thee, poet, and thy song;
Much comfort has each brought to me,
In days of sad uncertainty,
Through all these years along.
I love thy music more and more,
As to my soul the chords sound o'er;

Nor can I tell thee what I feel
When through my soul they softly steal,
But, oh! I would that thou couldst know
What grateful feelings outward flow.

—o—

MONEY.

MONEY is less than the least of all things
Left to Adam before or after his fall;
But a crumb from the sumptuous feast
Of blessings God-given to all;
Of possessions the smallest of small.
Fit to be used in a proper way,
Honestly, carefully, well:
Made a good servant, but never a lord
Unto the heart or the lip or the hand,
Else may it sear with its burning brand.

What can it buy?—for in keeping 'tis worthless,
Worse to be kept than the dust of the street—
Never a home nor a friend nor a lover;
Honor nor talent nor wisdom nor life.
What can it buy for the heart that is precious—
Comfort in sorrow or rest for the weary?
Nothing but houses and vanishing pleasures;
Nothing but things we must leave as we go;
Nothing but trifles too small for perfection,
Nothing eternal—ah! nothing, we know.

And from the man who an idol shall make it
Death shall demand all the flow'rs of his heart;

Wither and scorch them with gold-shine forever;
Burn up their petals with niter of silver;
Smother their fragrance in dim, dusty paper,
Till the whole man will be fashioned
From his head to his feet;
Formed by the breath and the throb and the beat
Of desire most insatiate
To have gold and keep it and hide it,—
Till his tenderness withers,
His home love decays,
And callous he grows; cold
As the money he worships and loves;
Till at length, without heart-friends,
He lies by the gold ore and silver
Down under the sod of the hill.

——o——

FRUSTRATED.

(To E.)

"The best laid schemes o' mice an' men
Gang aft a-gley."

Two rings of gold
Were given to me by a maiden fair,
Placed for a moment in my hand and care
Until she should return; and so I mused,
Turning the circlets o'er and o'er,
On sayings I had read before.

How everything
Comes down to us in circles round and round—

Light through the air or waves of pleasant sound;
How earth is but a spheroid which revolves
Itself, revolving round a ring,
As morning comes and evening!

How days and years
In winding circles ever come and go,
Inclosing for us either weal or woe!
How hills surround and blue skies arch,
While the horizon circleth all
Visible things upon this ball.

And so I wished,
Vainly I know, that I might learn from these
Two rings what would a doubting heart appease;
Learn what the pulses beat within the bands
Which circled them, and where each day
A dozen secrets came their way.

For I had read
How ancient gods, for pledge of loving care,
Had given rings made from their golden hair
To one they loved, which should a token be
Of blessings that would e'er descend,
In falling circles without end.

And more I read,
How rings once worn upon the finger, could
Secrets reveal to others if they would
Be pressed against the warm and beating pulse;
For, rushing currents from the heart
Bear messages to every part.

Then as I tried
But failed to learn what most I wished to know,
I let the ancient tales and fancies go,
Resolving then that I would give the maid
Only one ring, and to her say,
"One now, and one another day."

Yet when she came
Tripping so lightly, with extended hand
To make her just and reasonable demand,
Her blue eyes beaming, I forgot to say
A single word, but gave each ring
Without the power of questioning.

——o——

SUNNYSIDE.

"I remember, I remember
The house where I was born."

HOME of my boyhood days! how doth this heart
Quicken at thought of thee, and haste its work
Like one who suddenly remembers aught
Important, but forgotten in the midst
Of work more near. Slow pulses feel the thrill
And send a glow upon my cheek; my eyes
Grow liquid, and these hands are trembling now,
So much I love thy name, my Sunnyside!

And I must pause here, though my soul be full
Of other, later thoughts which press their weight
And crowd against the dreams of long ago;
Thoughts, recollections, dear remembrances

Of what shall never be again; of what
Lies like a beauteous valley in the past,
Hidden sometimes by shadowy mists, but now
Clear in the stream of memory's lucid light.

Here is the garden with its narrow path,
A path that wanders every whitherward—
Like wilful child that will not guided be—
Now under apple trees, and now between
Green walls of vines and eglantine, which reach
Over the way, and cast strange tracery
Of shade upon the daylight there. Beyond
Stretches the clover field where we could run,
A dozen children, playing hide and seek,
And not be found, while every rosy head
Of clover saw the place and would not tell,
But helped to shield us with its triple leaf.

Not far away, where cherry bushes grew
And bore the red choke-cherries high aloft,
We had our play-house, on a little knoll
With grassy sides. Here came we when white bloom
Fell o'er the plum trees like thin flakes of snow,
And tender spears of green pierced through the earth
On hill-sides everywhere, and May flowers thrust
Their fresh, sweet faces through the leafy mould;
When pussy buds of willow broke their shells,
And warmed their downy fur backs in the sun.
Here were we too when dandelions shot
Their yellow suns abroad o'er all the field,
And vi'lets, white and pink and yellow, hid
Their pretty modest faces by the brook;

And fire-weed flamed, and dear forget-me-nots
Made us kneel down and pay them homage there.

Here lived we when the grass had grown
As tall as we, and all the trees hung low
With apples, plums, and cherries black and red;
When dark-eyed autumn flowers grew on the slopes,
And corn-fields tossed their silken fringes loose
For us to braid, and pumpkins gave us seats.
We played we people were of consequence,
Women and men who had secured the things
Children so covet—knowledge of the world,
Stature and years, and, looking forward, found
Our joy in what was yet to come, as we
In later years, for this same joy, backwards
Must look. Our home was humble, but it seemed
A palace, for we furnished it with great
And costly draperies made from Fancy's loom.
Nothing we lacked but what we could supply
By wishing it, while little Nell, the wife,
Faithfully performed her household duties, like
Some matron who had lived nigh half her days
Toiling at home. Children my sisters were
To us—two girls, and oft a neighbor's child
Would be their brother, and thus add a third
To our already happy family.

Sometimes we wandered from our sheltered nook,
On to the mountain-side and through the fields
Of long, long grass, where blue flowers tossed their heads
Among the hay-seed tufts, and there, below,
Close to the ground, we picked the strawberry,

And picked and ate, painting each others' cheeks
And lips till they were crimson red ; then strüng
A dozen straws with berries large and soft,
And homeward went, a harvest in our hands.

Oft, too, when birching season came, we took
Our lunch and sought old Polette's road, which went
Winding along down to the river brink,
Through woods of birch– sweet woods of scented birch—
Wherein we peeled the white bark from the trees,
Scraping the rich, sweet, pulpy juice until
We filled our birchen dishes full, then turned
Up towards our Prospect hill, and rested there
Awhile, sitting on Rest stone, near which lay
The little grave-yard sleeping silently.
Yonder the wide fields spread, with cottages
Among the garden plots ; then miles of land,
Stretching far up against the horizon,
Their woods of hemlock dark and tamarack,
While, by the sloping side, the river flowed,
Bending its course to suit the rugged hill,
Till in the distance, like a silver thread,
In many folds it wound itself away.

Often we went down to the river's edge
When the red sun was reaching towards the west,
My love and I, and watched the deep, dark stream
Flow on between its rocky sides, and sa w
Upon its bosom all the sky, the clouds,
The tinted leaves of maple, beech, and birch,
Reflected in a beauteous miniature.
And on the moss-grown sides we sat to make

Baskets of burdock burrs, with pails and chairs,
Or what we wished, according to our mood.
Now we would tell the hour by blowing off
The dandelion-down, when every seed
That stayed upon the stem would count one hour.
Or with the lichen we would make a chain,
A necklace, or a ring, which Nell would keep

And wear because I made it and so willed.
Mats wove we of the pliant stems that grew
About the river's edge, and linden leaves
Were turned to aprons. There we played till Eve
Touched the dark hemlocks with her misty hand,
And warned us plainly of approaching night.

And oft we picked the May flowers in the spring,
And gathered violets by the laughing brook,
And filled our hands in balmy summer-time
With fire-weed stems, and showy buttercups,
And succory, and lilies pale and wan.

O Sunnyside, how far thy prospect lies
From me to-day! 'tis as the promised land
To Moses, beautiful but far away;
Seen only and not realized. But he
Who stood on Nebo's top could view a land
That was to be, while I am looking back
To what has been—a past that will return
Never, except in memory.

——o——

ST. JOHN'S CHURCH.

SILENT the little church, where once
So many at the beat of pulses came,

With burning soul and restless heart.
  Father and maiden, son and feeble dame,

To cry to God and honest men,
  How England's heavy hand now bore them down;
How tyranny was forcing them
  To break allegiance to the kingly crown.

See how they come from far away!
  Old men with tight-pressed lip and faces white,
Signs of a mental combat which
  Is but precursor of a fiercer fight.

Old women leaning for support;
  Mothers with infant crooning at the breast;
Maidens and lovers hand in hand,
  Breathless and eager, pausing not for rest.

The church grows crowded; every pew
  Gives room until no room for more;
The aisles are pressed, and on the steps
  Hundreds are seeking entrance at the door.

Who mounts the stair? Ah! one who brings
  A hush of silence like the still of death;
See, from all eyes how eagerly
  They watch the comer now with bated breath!

He speaks, and like electric flash
  His words conducted are to hearts of men!
Shock after shock they feel, and yet
  He strikes them with his tongue of flame again,

Then thunders out his voice, till old
  Men clinch their wrinkled hands and forward bend;

Till young men stand in zeal, and women weep,
And with the maidens sobbing voices blend.

"God made us all," the speaker says,
"And in his image made us every one,—
Not one above another, but
All equal sharers in his soil and sun.

"Must we submit to tyranny
And unjust laws," he cries with patriot breath;
"Men of my country, cry with me,
'O give me liberty, or give me death!'"

Over one hundred years have passed away
Since here these voices filled the throbbing air
With cries for freedom, yet they ring
Not only in my heart, but everywhere.

And as the sun sinks low, I hear
Within the church and from each humble tomb,
Voices of those who fought and died
To bring the light of freedom through our gloom.

Richmond, Va., May, 1881.

——o——

TO MY CONFESSOR.

YOU know my sins, and follies too;
You have them at your fingers' ends;
The only thing I have to do
Is pardon full and free to sue,
And then to make amends

Please to absolve me now, my dear,
  And I will from my ways desist;
How can I err when you are near,
Or, sweet girl, give you cause for fear,
  Or your kind will resist?

The down-glance from your eyes I feel
  Reach deep within me, like some gleam
That through the leaves will downward steal,
And brighten as it doth reveal
  The pebbles in the stream.

Those red lips are two ruby gates,
  From which kind words like angels come;
Where Love with Patience now debates,
While Love demurs and Patience waits,
  And wrath is stricken dumb.

They cannot chide, those lips, ah, no!
  Though worthy of all blame I be;
They only can forgive, and so
Full absolution soon, I know,
  They will vouchsafe to me!

Come, now, my love, give me your hand,
  So small, and warm, and dimpled o'er;
I swear by every oath's demand,
In this or any other land,
  That I will sin no more.

——o——

TO NELLIE.

OVER the field where you have scattered seed,
  Has fallen the rain,

And the sun hath shone in a time of need,
Nor shone in vain.

For tall blades have sprung and their blossoms burst
Over it, one by one,
Watered by rain-clouds and sacredly nursed
By a gentle sun.

But no one in fruit-time came, so the day
Of the harvest went past;
And the untouched fruit has fallen away
To the earth at last.

Now nothing is left but the hardened seed
In the dead fruit's heart;
Oh, tell me, my Nell, shall a life indeed
From such promise start?

——o——

MIDNIGHT.

'Tis midnight and no sleep,
No sleep, comes to my eyes;
Long have I lain awake
Watching the skies,

Watching vague waves of cloud,
Moving like ghosts of night
Over the moon's pale face,
Veiling her light.

How do they drift and drift
Onward so far away,

Going no whitherward,
Where can they stray?

Large grows my vision now,
Nothing but sky I see—
Nothing but clouds that pass
On silently.

—o—

THE LEADERS.

"*Nostram nunc accipe mentem.*"

SAVE us, O Lord! from pigmy men
Who cry and shout and shriek till hoarse,
With idle word and accent coarse,
Their little arguments again!

Small politicians who can talk
And spill their vain words in the air,
Which fall like soot-flakes everywhere,
And blacken all the way we walk.

Are men so low they must be shown
Their duty by such shallow fools;
Whose tongues are used like common tools,
Much more another's than their own?

Yet such but babbling babblers be,
Their noisy streams must soon run dry;
They sourceless are, nor by and by
Will their wild waters reach the sea.

O you who see and think and feel,
Who hold a part of God's great mind,

Trust not these faithless leaders blind,
Nor your own reason's laws repeal.

Ask Him who gave you minds, to give
You courage now to show their worth,
And make you, whom He blessed with birth,
Feel your existence as you live.

——o——

IN THE MAPLE WOOD.

WITHIN this shade of maple wood,
Where, at high noon, day scarce can penetrate,
Upon some knoll, in thankful mood,
How sweet to think and wait!

To listen to the happy birds,
Which flit with lightsome wing from tree to tree,
Singing a song too sweet for words,
A heavenly minstrelsy!

To watch the gentle flowers bend
In low obeisance to the passing breeze;
To see light's quivering arrows blend
Their points beneath the trees!

And dance upon the brooklet's breast,
Or lighten up the lily's ashen face;
Oh, bliss it is indeed, and rest
To be in such a place!

Yonder a winding path leads on,
O'ergrown and strewn with fallen leaf and seed,
Where, toiling from the early dawn,
The squirrel finds his meed,

And chatters gaily to himself
  At each discovery for his winter store,
Then scampers off like some wee elf,
  But yet returns for more!

Near by, a noisy bumble-bee
  Makes all the air with his own music ring;
And swiftly darting, I can see
  The dragon's double wing!

There, like a falling leaf, so white
  Floating, a butterfly sinks toward the stream,
Wherein, reflected by the light,
  It motionless doth seem.

I could live always with such things
  To charm my senses into dream-like rest,
For here sweet fancy taketh wings
  To grant my soul's request.

Now slant the rays of sinking sun,
  With no one near but quiet earth and me;
Soon will the fading day be done,
  And night fall silently.

O Earth! how rich thy treasures be
  In gifts to every creature great and small!
How doth my heart go out to thee,
  Thou mother of us all!

Home, August, 1883.

——o——

TO CAPTAIN L.

Est in secessu longo locus: insula portum
Efficit objectu laterum, quibus omnis ab alto
Frangitur, inque sinus scindit sese unda reductos.
—Virg. A. I. 159.

I.

ALL through the warp of life does sorrow weave
Its strange, dark threads, but still
We ply the shuttle of our will,

And weave across the fine white silk, and weave
Careful or careless, as we may,
The fabrics for another day.

II.

Of good our ills are made, and surely will
Prove good to us, if only we
Dissolve them with our Alchemy;

For nothing harmful is to him who knows
How to resolve the woe and pain
Back to their elements again.

The lack within us lies, and all is good
That comes to good men everywhere
Through water, fire, or earth, or air.

III

There is a place deep in the mind's recess,
A beauteous island of the soul,
Where safety is when waters roll

In tidal waves of trial and of wrong;
Or in the rising flow of pain
Which ebbs away and flows again.

Safely the island rests, and every wave
Raging against it breaks and swerves
Back on itself in falling curves.

And from the sea of trouble here below
Naught can affect that island's peace, for He
Holds its foundations in eternity.

EARLY PIECES.

TO MOTHER.

(With birthday greetings, April 26, 1881.)

THE Past with all her treasures, yet receives
Into her reaching lap another year;
While poorer Present loudly grieves,
And gathers her remaining sheaves,
As the wind gathers up the leaves.

Dim Future stern seems but a waste,
A desert stored with coming time.
Of which ne'er comes a sure foretaste
But which the Present takes with haste,
And holds about her with a pride sublime.

And then she writes before our face
Promises from this grim Future yet to be
Of some more years, some extra grace,
That may permit a longer race,
That soon alone the past will see.

Ah! Future, cold and haughty, now
I would not ask one single day;
For it is written on thy brow,
Of thy hard dealings oft, and how
Requests were granted in a cruel way.

Thou may'st have years of happy life
To give us all a part;
And then, perhaps, 'tis years of strife,
Where pain and sorrow ere are rife,
And aching wounds to bruise the heart;
So never do I ask thee aught,
And joy or sorrow coming, comes unsought.

Dear Past! for thou art always sad;
So full of many thoughts that seem
To fill thy soul and never make thee glad;
How oft thy face looks tho' there had
Come to thy mind some longing dream!

Happy to-day, child of the present hour,
I greet thee now, and humbly ask
Thee for one lasting, little flower
From out the many in thy bower,
To aid me in my loving task.

——o——

HOLD THOU MY HAND.

Saviour, the way is long and dark;
And when I see the waters drear
Angry and raging, almost I fear
With faith so small my little bark
Will sink.

Guide thou me it and keep it safe
From every tossing wave of ill
And danger; help me to do thy will

And serve thee more,—not like the waif
  Wander away,

But in thy love serve thee alone,
And praise the Maker of my life,
In joy or sorrow, pain or strife,
Praise yet to thee, my God, alone
  For all.

Oh! help me trust and never doubt
Of anything that thou hast said—
Just read thy word as some have read
And trust,—not think a thought about
  The rest.

Faith gave the Elders good report;
So through this faith we die one death
To live again, as Scripture saith,
To join an everlasting court
  Of light.

Do I not know that He is just,
And on that dreadful day will know
His jewels; and sever from below,
From sin all who did calmly trust
  His word?

Then I may know, for saith the Lord divine,
"I, I will spare my jewels in that day,
Those who have followed in my way;
Those precious jewels shall be mine
  In Heaven."

Father, my only dearest Friend,
Press thou my hand and keep it firm,

For I am weak—a feeble worm,
Apt to be crushed—and then not lend
My aid,
For I would have thee tightly hold my hand,
That I may walk in confidence, and teach
Others of thy dear love; help them to reach
Our home, that beauteous, far-off land,
Of rest.

I walk, and as I go light is around,
And joy, and peace—all gladness in my heart;
I would not from the path depart,
But of the precious peace I have
Impart,
And spread it on from land to land,
Fill every man with God's own love,
Give him that mission from above,
That he may join the happy band
And sing
Loud with the psalmist of God's heart,
Praise ye the Lord, 'tis good to sing
Praises of love to our great King,
For he is great, and rules above,
Commanding nature at his will,
E'en telling oceans to be still,
And yet he is a God of love
And merciful.

——o——

1879.

TRUE FRIENDS.

WE know some friends are found
Around

Us, like the stones upon the ground,
Which, clustered o'er the fields away,
  Do stay.

But true friends are not ever found
  Around;
They are like diamonds 'neath the ground,
Which hold well hidden in the earth
  Their worth.

Among the stones upon the field
  Revealed,
Some shine out like the burnished shield,
And some like precious gems of gold,
  Untold.

But the bright treasures in the mould,
  All gold,
Will never of themselves unfold;
They must be sought for, and are found
  Fast bound.

——o——

LINES.

[On receiving a bunch of magnolia leaves from a distant friend.]

LEAVES fresh and green,
Have you sent to me;
They come, I ween,
From the dear old tree
That stood in the sun with nitid leaves,
And caught all the rain drops from the eaves;

That whispered and sang, as through and through
Its branches the musical South wind blew.

They seem to tremble and shake again,
As they did before in the wind and rain,
And the thoughts of dear days crowd through my
brain;
I am thinking, loved friend so good and true,
Of the precious days that I spent with you,
Of a weary coming so gladly met,
Of gentle kindness that lingers yet,
Of a child watched over with patient care,
Of impulses deep laid open and bare,
Of waiting till sickness and woe went by,
Of watching the dark clouds from the sky,
Of bidding at last a long adieu,
Of seeing each other fade from view,
One in the city and one on the blue.

I see the strange, strange little town,
With its homely houses low and brown,
And I hear the rush on that rough old quay
Where you stood alone and beckoned to me;
I beckoned back,
I beckoned again,
But I could not stay, and my tears were vain.
I remember well, when my tears were dry,
I watched the city sink into the blue,
And the tall, tall palm trees against the sky
Were sentinels guarding your isle, I knew,
As the spires of the churches stood up between
Their graceful forms of brown and green.

Now when the winds blow in your tropic clime,
And wondrous flowers bud out in pride sublime,
    With petals of white
    In the sunny light;
When your shining leaves smile back to the sun,
Or catch the dews when the day is done,
    I will gaze upon this,
    My beautiful treasure,
    And drink a full measure
    Of memory's bliss.

1882.

———o———

FIDUS ACHATES.

(To N.)

ALMOST a life
  Of friendship, that to me
Was very true and dear,
  Has ceased to be.

And for a word
  I cannot now recall,
Love I have told thro' years
  Must wear its pall.

An ache, a pain
  Throbbing against my heart,
That needs the sympathy
  It doth impart.

A cruel wound
  For which is there no cure

But time? O Time! soon make
  Thy healing band secure.

And yet the hand
  That brought the flowing blood,
All stained,—I would but wet
  And wash it with a tearful flood.

Who would have said
  That in the after years,
Our friendship and our love,
  Would bring us cause for tears?

What child would think
  When the fair sun is bright,
That a few little hours
  Shall bring the dark of night!

That summer warmth,
  And the sweet flow'rets gay,
Will in a few short weeks
  Vanish and fade away!

Or that the sea,
  Calm as some mountain lake,
May soon dash angry waves
  And make its islands shake!

Oh, what will time
  Not ever dare to do—
Changing flowers, sea, or sun,
  And friendships dear and true?

Pray, friend, that we,
  In our firm friendship now,

May never have to wear
Its thorns upon our brow.

Oh! make it then
So very near thy heart
That years, with all their wiles,
May never make us part.

Some things change not,
And why need our love change?
Oh! why need time or age
Our trustful hearts estrange?

——o——

FOLLOW ME.

(JOHN 1 : 43.)

"DEAR Lord," I said, "I cannot go;
Cans't thou not give me other work to do?
My hands are feeble and my feet too slow.

"I know my offerings have been small,
But thou, O Lord, with goodness unsurpassed,
Hast taken, and with blessing paid them all.

"But if I go unto those lands
Far, and away from all I know or love,
Will strength enough uphold these trembling hands?

"Could I not labor here as well,
Teach some, and learn from others as I teach,
Gaining in power and might thy love to tell?"

"My child," and not in anger said,
A voice did answer wondrous kind and sweet,
"Must I yet tell thee o'er what thou hast read?

"About the fishermen of old,
How they made answer to my 'Follow me,'
Gave all they had to give, nor sought, nor sold.

"More, too, they left,—family and all,
Treading with patient feet the thorny path,
Not even fearing what might yet befall.

"Many a thorn tore the soft flesh
Of their too tender feet, while the blood flowed
As does the juice from fruit that broken is, and fresh.

"Oft new-healed wounds were torn again,
And nature's acts roughly undone,
Leaving behind a trail of crimson stain.

"But yet they followed me, until
White locks were crowns of glory that they wore,
And their knees trembled as they followed still.

"Gird up thy loins with faith, my child;
Thou art my servant, and I ask of thee
To help us glean our harvest from the wild.

"For fields are white, wasting away,
And hoary heads bend low like ripened grain,
To fall and die, if we provide no other way.

"Nations in darkness reach to me,
And call for what they would but know not of,
Striving in weary bonds for liberty.

"And unto you who now are free,
To all rejoicing in my love,
I ask to tell the tale of Calvary.

"I will uphold thee, do not fear,
My strength sufficient is for all thy needs;
I will watch o'er thee and be ever near.

"The ignorant have I made wise,
And to the feeble I have given strength,
And filled with hope the heart that knew but sighs.

"Tongues that were ever slow of speech
Have I made full of words and truth and fire;
And those as babes in learning 'apt to teach.'

"My ways are not the ways of man,
And so my laws must ofttimes differ from
E'en thy sincere and well-intentioned plan.

"Therefore fail not; I bid thee go
And whisper in that Nation's ear the truth,
That I am Him 'from whom all blessings flow.'

"And I will be to thee a God,
Loving thee as I loved my Israel,
Withholding oft the chastening of the rod.

"Depart, and do not tarry long
In this place; follow me to the land
Where I have promised thou shalt soon belong.

"Depart, the sun sends up his light
Already from the eastern horizon,
And when he sees the west, it will be night.

"Depart far out to that dark land,
While yet thy life is in its eastern glow,
That, sinking to the West, it shall be grand.

"Depart, thou shalt not find a king
More just to guide his people as they go
Far from their home, or grant them anything.

"At last I will not say, 'Depart,'
But, 'Welcome, child, to thy eternal home,'
Granting the holy wishes of thy heart.

"For I will give thee lasting rest
From all that ever caused thee pain or woe,
And an abode among the blissful blest."

"I will not tarry, my dear Lord,
Nor ask for other work that is not mine,
But do as thou hast bid, trusting thy word.

"Strengthen my hands, oh! make them strong
To carry tidings heavy with thy love,
And bear them bravely as I pass along.

"Direct my steps aright, my King,
And keep them from the way not sure or safe,
And from the tempting paths that ruin bring.

"So farewell all! I go far hence,
Taking my Master's hand and leaning hard,
Looking with hope up to the firmaments,

"And wondering if I still may look
Upward from earth to those small, shining stars,
When many years have turned life pages in my book;

"Or whether these same stars will shine
Upon my grave instead, while I am far
Above them and rejoicing in a light divine.

"It may be One will watch from earth,
While one with love watches from Heaven,
Longing to welcome there another birth.

"It will be well, and His way best,
Whether we toil long years, or wing
Gladly a flight to our supernal rest.

"One has gone there before us all,
And she will look and smile upon us, when
We hasten to obey the Master's call."

———o———

A GUEST.

I KNOW not why, this night my grief
Has all returned to me;
My heart aches sore, and for relief
Hot tears fall heavily.

Sorrows that burst long years ago
Like dark waves over me,
Are here to-night, but ebb and flow
Their waters silently.

I wonder much. Soul, dost thou know?
But list! a voice I hear:
"Grief is not subject to the will,
Nor reason's mind austere.

"Thy grief thou canst not ever hide,
It heeds no sacrifice;
No woe of thine has ever died,
For no great sorrow dies.

"It may lie buried in the breast
Through weeks and months and years,
When, like some unexpected guest,
It suddenly appears,

"Yet welcome is, though bringing pain
And ache and mental rack;
Though to thy soul it once again
Bring such sad memories back."

Then welcome to my heart, O friend!
Take all I hold as mine;
I will not stand aloof, but bend
My wish and will to thine!

1878.

———o———

HOW THE WATER-LILY CAME.

On a sunny day in the month of May,
A May-flower and a Lily met;
Their faces were bright in the morning light,
And their cheeks with the dew were wet.

"Well," said the flow'r, "at this early hour,
'Tis good we are here, my friend;
I am sure that we, if you agree,
May together our pleasure blend."

The Lily blushed and with cheeks a-flushed
  So modestly answered, " Yes,"
That the May-flower stood in the shady wood,
  With a heart full of tenderness,

And he put down his face with a pleasing grace,
  As he whispered into her ear,
"Let us go to King May on this summer day
  And be wed this very year."

So hand in hand through the woody land,
  They went to the King of May;
But sternly he said: "You can never wed
  That Lily, as you say.

"We May-flowers are so very far
  Above the common race,
That I must brand your strange demand
  As exceeding out of place."

And the haughty king saw each trembling thing
  Bow at his cruel look;
But he uttered the word, and never stirred
  As his palace they forsook.

So on they sped, for they would wed,
  Whatever the king might say,
Till they came to a stream where a merry gleam
  Led into a pleasant way.

But all seemed foes, and of their woes
  Did not care to hear them tell;
How they met, and love from its flight above
  Had come in their hearts to dwell.

At last they came to a blind old dame,
Who lived by the water's side;
Her face was yellow, but soft and mellow,
And her hands were smooth and wide.

Then, growing bold, the May-flower told
Of his love for the Lily maid;
How the King of May, that very day,
Had refused to lend them aid.

But the Lily cried, "I can be your bride,
For the king is far away;
And I surely think, at this brooklet's brink,
We should let our hearts be gay."

Now the blind old dame was known to fame,
And secrets of men she told;
By snapping a pod she became a god,
And wise as a sage of old.

To the Lily she said, "Your life I have read
By the lines in your pretty face;
Here is the bend where your troubles end,
This is your resting-place.

"Not many days hence will some bright days commence,
For a son shall inherit your name;
And an honor will he to his country be,
Yea, bring you a lasting fame."

So saying she took a leaf from her book
And gave to the Lily fair;
Her book was a rose that blossoms and blows,
With color and fragrance rare.

Then she made them a boat, and in it they float,
  On the calm of a rippling lake;
As they merrily play and laughingly say,
  "Let us now of this beverage take."

As soon as they drink, the dame gives a wink,
  And the lake sinks them into its breast,
Where away from all dross they sink to the moss,
  And partake of the pleasure of rest.

"Oh, happy the day when we followed the way
  That led to this gay retreat!"
And they sang to the mosses, which, with vain little tosses,
  Laughed back in their voices so sweet.

Now the Lily looked wise, and a light in her eyes
  Betokened the end of their mission;
For her mind was at rest, and in it imprest
  The leaflet's wondrous commission.

Soon, Lucina came down to the watery town,
  And attended the birth of one
Who was fair as the rose—though in water he grows,
  While he lifts up his face to the sun.

The mosses were gay, and, in royal array,
  Shouted loud at the birth of a prince;
For he rose to the top of the rippling drop,
  And has smiled to the sun ever since.

Now they sleep 'neath the mosses, and the water-lid tosses
  His head in the shining sun;
And he bears on his breast the picture and crest
  Of those whose journey is done.

If ever you float in your pleasure-boat,
  And come to a Lily fair,
Just ask for his history, and the wonderful mystery
  He will tell with a pleasing air,

How he came to be named and so wonderfully famed;
  How his beauty is never surpassed;
His mother was Lily, and he, Water-lily,
  Has been called from the first to the last.
1878.

——o——

AT EVENING.

'TIS autumn evening, and the sun,
Fast sinking, tells his work is done;
Great cumulous clouds are colored bright
With many shades of varying light,
And hills and mountains throw their shadows o'er
A grassy meadow or some cottage door.
Across the fields they move and still keep on,
Until the fading day's last beam is gone;
Until the mountains, wrapt in sombrous night,
Spread like huge giants up against the light.
Now, far beyond, the sun sends up its smile,
Which here and there the golden clouds beguile;
And near the sun, above the forest green,
Small specks of gold and silver may be seen,
Which move, like visions in the eye of man,
That shine, then fade, and then shine out again.
The earth is silent, all her voice is still;

The ploughman rests his steed; and at the mill
Waters, now unrestrained, rush to their course,
And seek a pebbly bed with murmur hoarse.
Soon as the lighter clouds are gone,
Huge forms, fantastically drawn,
Hover about the darkened earth
And wreathe it with a horizontal girth.
Above, the heavens shine out in twinkling dots,
As though some painter carelessly made spots
By shaking paint into the spreading blue,
The first ones larger and of whiter hue,
Then others smaller, till at last, in play,
He shakes his brush and forms the Milky Way.
The moon is absent from the starry vault,
Because--in very truth a dark cloud's fault—
She screens her face, and from us hides the light,
That soon would chase the timid shades of night.
But see! she bolder grows with longing face,
And casts her veil into another place.
Quickly weird forms of shadow shyly glide
By forests dense or to the mountain-side,
And some to other places turn their feet,
Fast, faster yet, for light is very fleet,
Thus do they flit and flee or now return,
As the mild guardian of these hours may learn
The inner secrets of a cautious night,
And change its gloomy spirits into light.

'Tis autumn every year, and oftener, too,
The sun goes down, shades come, and stars shine true.
Oh! should we not thank God for such a sight

As fading sunset and a starry night;
Intelligence to read those distant spheres,
And earth's relation to them all in rolling years?
For when we sit beneath God's wondrous sky,
To view his work—stupendous work on high—
We with the psalmist would rejoice and say,
How excellent is His name from day to day,
Night unto night shows knowledge of his power,
Nor speech nor language can above it tower.

———o———

TO M. J. A. P.

My friend, our village poet,
  Unto thee I sing this song.
Wilt thou hear it? Wilt thou take it?
  For it doth to thee belong.

Oft have I admired thy music,
  Chords and harmonies so sweet,
And thy soft and gentle rhythm
  So with joy my heart doth greet,

That I cannot keep from singing,
  Cannot keep thee from thy praise,
But with pleasure in the duty
  Would mine Ebenezer raise.

Young art thou, but there is promise
  Thou wilt sing the poet's lays,
Which will bring thee to remembrance
  In the long and future days.

Strains will echo from thy mountains
 And resound along the bays,
With a soft reverberation
 Up our steep, romantic ways,

And some day we may be singing
 Songs that claim their birth from thee;
Reaching back in their returning
 Like some loved and lost *Ami.*

Though thy flowers be few in number,
 We have promise still of more;
For the plant that blossoms early
 Always keeps some buds in store,

And these buds will surely blossom,
 Ope their petals wide—and send,
Out to every land and nation,
 Fragrance from my poet friend.

So in parting I would thank thee
 Once again, and then farewell,
But remember that thy name is
 In the land of song to dwell.

Quebec, 1879.

——o——

I DID NOT KNOW.

DEATH, I can greet thee now, and gladly take thy hand,
That leads so far down in the narrow way,
Through the drear valley, to the other land.

Once I did shudder at the thought that this grim death
Some day would lead me to himself, and take
This beating life, my soul, and all my breath.

And oft, when nearing to the twilight hour, or night,
Sad thoughts would tell my heart their secrets o'er,
And dwell upon the parting, and life's fight;

How some, though weary of their own existence,
When came, at last, the awful gloom of death,
Would seek to live, and struggle in resistance;

Then, looking at our earth, more firmly would I say,
"I cannot leave my home -- this happy world—
For death—that world of darkness—not a day."

I loved to think about the land of pearly gates,
As something far and ever out of reach,
Held deep within the womb of future fates.

But for myself, I loved the world, its pomp and show,
The empty pleasures which it gives, and short,
Because God's lesson yet I did not know.

All is not told thee why I do not fear death more,
But long to see him take his hour-glass up
Firmly, and say, "Prepare, thy course is o'er."

All would be more than thou couldst wish to hear,
Of agonizing sorrow, grief, and pain;
Loss of my home, and what, I pray, more dear?

A husband lay upon his bed in feverish dreams;
His children two, and mine, nearing the end,
That reached them just before the morning beams.

Death entered, and without a note of warning
Marked on his glass the measure of each life,
And took them all, my very own, ere morning.

How did I pray and plead that I might keep but one,
But still relentless heard he not my voice,
Leaving me broken-hearted at the rising sun.

When weary eyes so full of light not long ago,
Closed with the constant pleading of the pain,
My heart no more withstood; I knelt, bowed low.

I did not weep a flood of tears, but sadly knelt
Down by the side of my departed own
In agony, not knowing what I felt.

And then I prayed to Him who brings all lasting peace,
That He would calm my proud, rebellious heart
With rest from sources that can never cease.

God gave me peace and hope, that blissful hope
Which faith and trust and love only can bring,
And which enlarged my vision and my scope.

I know full well pain went not from my heart that day,
God knows the aching void I felt for years
Succeeding, but I knew God's better way.

Now, many years have passed away; they still go on,
And speed me onward to eternity,
As shadows fall upon me, ere the dawn.

Still there is pleasure in the thought, "I'm going home,"
And that my Master needs me here no more
To toil alone, to sorrow, or to roam.

And what a glorious greeting when I reach the land;
Past all temptation, and all weary pain;
Led through the journey safe by his right hand!

A strong and guiding hand will surely lead me on,
Keep all my steps; while little hands of love
Will lighten burdens till the night is gone.

Now dost though wonder yet, when all my work is done,
That I should wish, and watch, and wait alway,
For death to tell me that my race is run?

For, nearing to the twilight hour, or night,
Sweet thoughts will tell my heart their secrets o'er,
And dwell upon the meeting and life's flight.

——o——

TO MY BROTHER.

[On his birthday.]

Do you remember—ah! how could you forget—
Those sacred evenings when the sun had set,
That recess high and small beneath the attic stairs
Where we were wont to creep oft unawares;
And where the hours did glide so fast, when evening came
It caught us building castles great in airy fame?
How many did we build, how great, how high,
False pictures of the misty by and by!
Then twilight hour would catch us there to add anew;
We would be noble knights who bravely thousands slew;
With sword and shield we fought like bloody men,
Or lived like pirates in some gloomy den.

But ever when we spoke of deeds we should not do,
Conscience would smite us hard and better feelings woo;
Remind us of the very things we knew,
That better was the good man than the one who slew.
Or when grim shadows made our récess dark as night,
Knowing our former themes were wrong, we turned them
right,
And talked of being men of truth and valor strong,
Who fought, if need be, to resist the wrong.
And you remember Sabbaths, how they passed!
Those days, when we must do our duty plain,
Learn Bible verses, and, forgetting, learn again,
Until dear mother, satisfied we knew them well,
Would bid us sit and listen while she'd tell,
Not tales of wild adventure, but of old;
Of David, of the temple and its gold!
These were our romances; of Joseph would we hear,
His childhood and captivity—his father's fear.
And when she told of Jesus, oh! better far than all,
Our hearts would throb. Why should they give him gall?
We would exclaim with earnest, flowing tears.
It touched us then—our hearts were tender as our years.
Why can we not e'er live in childhood and enjoy
Pleasures like these—as free from all alloy?
Why should each year bring with it added care,
And make this world to us less kind and fair?
His will it is. Time speeds us on and on;
Obey we must, to find that youth is gone;
Each birthday comes, leaving one year behind,
Which passes from us like a sad thought from the mind.
And thus in youth, glad days, we longed to be

Sailors on life's wild, boisterous sea.
The time is now, and our fond dreams we meet,
Perhaps as men of valor, but with feeble feet.
Our knights of youth are gone, our castles high
Flown from us like the nervous butterfly,
And though we realize the dreams of being men,
Little are they like dreams when you were ten;
And age must come, and childhood pass away,
For time is fleeting and our life a day.

—o—

IN A SCHOOL-MATE'S ALBUM.

SHOW your true colors, and the flag unfurl
Of your just Principle. Into the wind
Free let it wave, and o'er the lightnings fierce
Of Opposition. If drops of rain do,
Falling from Slander's cloud, now make it droop,
Soon as the storm bursts loud the flag will spread
Abroad its folds, shaking the rain from off
Their colors bright, and show how they were made
More fair and bright for their slight dampening.
1877.

—o—

THE TWO ROADS.

Two roads are ever ready
For travelers who know not the way,
Each leads through a lonely valley,
And one to a pleasant city;

Both guide to an endless day.
And the road that leads to the city
Is plain with His smile o'er the way,
But the other is ever leading
Its many far out and astray.

1879.

——o——

NICODEMUS.

THERE was a man, a Pharisee,
A learnéd one and wise,
Who came to Jesus and by night
Inquired of him for the precious light
That never dies.

And Jesus, willing then, as now,
Told him the story o'er,
How that he, and every sinful man,
To be free from sin must be born again,
As once before.

But the wise and learned ruler
Knew not what Jesus said,
For, doubting yet, he could not see
How now or ever these things could be
That he never read.

And He still tells on the story
In his word to us each day,
Pointing, with love and pity
Up to the wondrous city,
A way

That leads to a grand old city,
Where many mansions be,
With shining streets of heavenly gold,
Where all can His dear face behold
And see.

1879.

APPLE BLOSSOMS.

PRETTY apple blossoms,
Blossoms pure and fair,
Sending luscious fragrance
Through the morning air,

Make me think of snow-flakes
Covering all the trees,
Dropped in dire confusion
By some careless breeze.

Here and there a pink bud
Hides its modest face,
Then, unfolding slowly
With a beauteous grace,

Opens wide its petals
To our wondering view,
And becomes a blossom
Perfect, full, and true.

Let away one summer
With its pleasant sun,
And the apple blossom's
Little life is done.

While, instead, great apples,
  Green and red and brown,
Turn their fair cheeks toward you,
  Asking to come down!

——o——

TWO SOLILOQUIES.

[Which have not yet reached the ears of Cupid and Opportunity.]

HE.

I LOVE a lass so very much,
  I think a lass loves me.
I have no courage to express
  That love; has she?

SHE.

That funny boy, I love him well;
  He seems to love me too,
And were I in his place—I know
  What I should do.

——o——

TO MAY.

I KNOW a pretty maiden,
  Whose large blue eyes
Do often make me think
  Of summer skies!

As bright and clear they look,
  As far and deep,

Hiding from busy Time
 The thoughts they keep,

Which, if they're like her eyes,
 I now would know,
What fairer thoughts than these
 Could live below.

Sometimes clouds come and make
 Tears fall like rain;
But then the sun soon comes
 And shines again.

I hope few clouds may pass
 O'er those blue eyes,
Like some which often vex
 The summer skies;

But may they always be
 Free from a care,
And see the world as kind
 As they are fair.

——o——

IN AN ALBUM.

MANY are the years which come,
 And many the ones that go;
Upon our hearts in this rolling time,
 Shall the light of our friendship glow?

DE GOOD OLE DAYS.

I'SE ole an' gray,
An' de only way
I spen' de hours dat go,
Am to tink ob de days when I were young,
Of de kin' ole peepil I libbed among,
Of de days dat come no mo'.

Fer dis hair am white,
An' de glory light
Dat shine on de earf an' you,
Am darker to me dan my niggah skin;
No nebber a gleam ob it do shine in,
Not a speck ob de light shine froo.

I would lub to see
Jess one bush or tree
Ob de big plantation groun',
Dat I wo'k upon in dose happy days
When de darkeys sung all de sweetes' lays,
An' play wid de merr-go-roun'.

Ole Massa he come,
An' fetch de big drum
In de ev'nin' when we dance,
An' Sambo an Mose play de violeen—
Oh! dat were the pretties' sight I seen,
To see all the niggahs prance!

Dere war Chlo an' Moll,
My Dinah an' Poll;

Dere war Pete an' Sam an' Jo,
Dese all war my friends—but de udder ban's
Come togedder, and soon we all joins han's—
Dere war Roosh an' many mo'.

Den massa would say,
"Now come dis way,
You hab dance enuff to-night;
Here am good sweet candy for one an' all,
Help you'selves to 'lasses, bof great and small,
And each pull wid all tha might."

How we pull an' tear
Done stick up our hair,
An' run all de 'lasses dry,
An' den we sit down by the moonlight an' sing
Dem deah ole songs dat still does ring,
Fit enuff to make me cry.

An' now when I tink
My ole heart do sink,
An' teahs comes into my eyes,
Fer Dinah, my wife, an' de udder fren's
Is gone an' am singin' da sweet amens
In dat lan' beyond de skies.

An' I bress de Lord
An' his holy word
Dat I'll see de light once mo',
Dat he'll gib me soon dat fair lan' to see,
Where all my deah niggah fren's 'll be,
Dat lan' on the udder sho'.

Fer I'se ole an' gray,
An' de ondly way
I spen' de hours dat go,
Am to tink ob de days when I were young,
Ob the kin' ole peepil I libbed among—
Ob de days dat come no mo'.

Danville, Va., November, 1881.

——o——

COME 'LONG, SINNAH.

COME 'long, sinnah,
  Come an' be save',
Ef you doan do it,
  You's goin' to de grave.
De Lord his arm am mighty,
  De Lord his lub am great,
An ef you ondly ax him,
  You'll nebber hab to wait.

Come 'long, sinnah,
  Oh! doan delay,
Jesus am waitin',
  An' mebby he can't stay,
Fer he hab odder bus'ness
  Dat call him roun' de globe,
An' now's de time to gib him
  Ycu' order fer a robe.

Come 'long, brudder,
  What am you 'bout,
All de days you hab
  E'll soon be runnin' out,
An' all de souls you's leavin'
  To go along in sin,
Will poun' de gates ob Hebben
  Fer you to let dem in.

Den, O brudder!
  What'll you say,
When all dose sinnahs
  From Hebben's kep' away?
I tink you will be wishin'
  Wid all your might an' main
Dat massa, he would gib you
  One little chance again.

You, too, sistah,
  What am you' song?
You to de minstrels
  Ob Hebben does belong,
An' dis yere am you' mission
  To sing de jubilee;
To tell de worl' from bondage,
  De Lord hab set it free.

Columbia, S. C., 1881.

——o——

AS WE GWINE TURNIN' ROUN'.

DEY tells us dat dis earf am roun'
  An' ervolves in de air,

Turnin' an' turnin', but I believe
  Dat dis yere am not fair,
An' we could nebber hab got heah
  Widout some climbin' stair.

De idee dat ou' Lord would put
  Us on a rollin' ball,
An' let us scramble to ou'selves
  Wid likelerhood to fall,
Am not de way to keep his own,
  I does not tink, at all.

Ef dat be so, de Lord know when
  De watahs ob de sea,
Might come a-swoopin' all about
  To swalla you an' me;
An' also would de Lord know whar
  De res' ob us would be?

I'se gwine to tell you dis, my fren',
  Dat settle all de case,
Dere am in ole Kentucky State
  A mighty lastin' place,
Dat all de movin' ob de globe
  Hab nebber yet deface'.

De house hab stan' dere fer a time
  Dat you an' me can't name,
An' ef you goes dar you will fin'
  It's stan'in' jess de same.
I knows dis talk about de earf
  Am all a bluffin' game.

Dat's so—de ole house nebber could
  Hab stuck on to de groun,'
Fer ebbery stone were loose an' would
  Be shu' to tumble down,
Jess when dey reach de under side
  As we gwine turnin' roun'.

TRANSLATIONS.

——o——

MARGUERITE.

[From the French of Madame Jenna.]

"In the morning, Margaret,
When the fields with dews are wet,
Tell me, as you dreaming go,
And against the flowers below
Press you close your brow of snow;
Tell me what unto the flower
You are whispering every hour?"
"This I whisper: 'Holy gift!
Broken from celestial rift,
Beautiful and silent star;
Though thine odors reach afar,
Happier far than lot of thine
Is this happy lot of mine,
For I hold a heart divine!'"

"What say you now, Margaret,
To the brook that murmurs yet,
And invites you to a seat
On its banks, where waters fleet
Hurry by with music sweet?"
"This I say: 'O ribbon stream!
Singing voice of living dream,

On whose crystal bosom shine
Reed, and bud of eglantine;
Willow branch, and insect bright,
Pictured there by ray of light,
Happier am I far than thou;
God with reason did endow
Her who speaketh to thee now!'"

"What words now, my Margaret,
Say you to the birds that flit
From the village to the tree;
From these banks to foot-paths free?
Speak to them and then to me."
"All I say is, 'Faithful friends
Of mankind and flower, ye send
Out your wings in every place
With a quick and easy grace;
All your song is free from sighs,
In your breasts no sorrows rise,
But more happy far than ye—
I shall live eternally.'"

——o——

DUST TO DUST.

[From the French.]

I.

Dust to dust,
Iron to rust,
Soon shall crumble and fall
Into mould and decay,

And vanish away,
Yea, all.

  Blades of grass,
  Pillars of brass,
Mountains of rugged rock,
Trees that grow high and tall,
Creatures both great and small
That walk

  Or that fly,
  Under the sky,
All shall wear into dust;
All shall dissolve the same,
Be what they may in name,
And rust.

  Loved things here
  Shall disappear,
And from our poor sense go;
Death around all the earth
Closely has drawn its girth
Of woe.

II.

Nothing that is shall cease to be,
Nothing through all eternity;
Dust or iron, or birds that fly,
Nothing that liveth beneath the sky,
  Blades of grass,
  Pillars of brass:
All shall be that e'er has been,
Somewhere, somehow, hid or seen;
Nothing shall die, though change is writ
Into life and over it.

FRAGMENT.

[From the French.]

AM I like those yellow leaves, cried I,
Which are falling to wither, and fade and die?
Shall I crumble to dust like them, and stay
Only a part of the earth's decay?

And a voice deep within me did then reply,
"Man, why dost thou question thus? oh, why?
For know there is in thee a soul which must
Rise higher than earth, or death, or dust;
'Tis an essence from God and ne'er can it die,
Though the casket that holds it in clay shall lie."

——o——

GOD.

[From the French.]

OF God's eternity do all things tell.
If depths we see not, shall we them ignore?
All nature sings his never-ending power,
And, with its voicing heart, bids us adore.

——o——

THE SWEET NIGHTS.

[From the Spanish.]

SWEETLY the sweet nights come
And sweetly they go,
Like strains of some music, soft and low;
While outward we follow with senses numb,

We are going, we know,
But our voices are dumb;
And we never return,
Though the sweet nights come.

——o——

ARCANA.

[From the French.]

O PRETTY cheeks, whose dimples deep
Now in sweet pink nests snugly sleep.
Do but awaken, and your smile
Will every human heart beguile!
O beaming eyes! pray tell me why
In your dark orbs such myst'ries lie!
And tell me, too, ye red, red lips,
Your chapters of Apocalypse!

——o——

APHORISM.

[French.]

HE who to live aright doth try,
Will live aright, and so will die.

——o——

FAITH.

TRUSTING the Lord
Thy faith will grow;
His will thy will shall be,
And thou shalt know,
Through every trial, every woe,
Full perfect peace below.

FLORIDIANA.

——o——

[A Medley.]

FOR Mexico did lave
With her soft wave
  Our prow;
While we, a jolly crew,
Who each the other knew,
Talked, sang, or read,
Then sank the lead,
To find how deep
Some waters sleep.
Sometimes we cast our eyes afar,
Over the waste of waters blue,
And saw there often what we knew
Would soon our peaceful sailing mar,
The nucleus of a squall,
Clouds large and dark,
Frowned on our bark,
In ominous threat of what us might befall.
And so we moved on toward the nearer shore,
Lest we the unknown farther need explore.

Then no church bell
Would toll our knell!
How sad 'twould be for us to feel
That we had known the last of weal,
And that we all must give our lives,
For others who would take our wives,
And gobble up our real estate
As fish do gobble up the bait,
But find the hook, alas, too late!
Now did our fattest man
Step to the bank;
Gaily along he ran
Holding the frying pan,
Sign of his rank.
"Anchored at last," one said,
As he looked overhead
Into the sky,
Saying that the false wind
Had quickly changed its mind,
As women do,
To trouble brew.
This spake our Boston man,
Who bore a Southern tan,
This and some more,
Which to your ears, we may,
If you are willing, tell some day.

CANTO I.

[*Dolce far niente.*]

In style befitting
We were sitting

Under some waving trees,
While summer bees
Buzzed all about our ears,
And oft aroused our fears,
Yet did not deign to sting,
Or threaten anything.
Near by the streets with sand were filled,
Since Tampa's mayor had calmly willed
That he would ever let them be
Loose samples of antiquity.

Weary one day of idle ease,
Of sitting under shady trees,
We took advantage of the breeze,
And started up on Tampa's stream
In a small skiff, wherein a scheme
We set about to ventilate.
Far up the river,
Where tall reeds shiver,
And water-turkeys shake their sides;
Where alligators show their hides,
And other ugly things besides,
We took our way, floating along,
Like echoes of some merry song.
Bananas grew on every side,
Pine-apples sent their fragrance wide,
While the fair orange glistening from its tree
Was now a beauteous thing to see;
Now here and there a stately pair
Of palm trees kept each other company.
There the guava, with its slim white waist,

Made us think how guavas taste,
And the odd mangrove whose strange roots are seen
As waters pass beneath them and between.
'Twas up the Lockapopka stream
Where we were floating like a dream,
Restful but real, until we came
To one called Benjamin by name,
Who had a boat
That well could float
On any river or on sea,
With quite becoming dignity.
This did he aptly call the *Pet*,
Because its sides had oft been wet
With spray and foam,
When, tossing on the waters gay,
It courage kept, though far from home.
Many the time its helm was cast
Into the great and moving vast,
When creaking cord and straining mast
Could scarce resist the coming blast;
But the brave *Pet*
Continued yet,
And soon became a favorite.
But now she lay upon her side,
As some were painting her in colors gay,
That she might once more sail away.
Ah, what a sun shone out that day!
So warm and bright, yet did not say,
"You must not work while I am out,"
But kindly let us move about.
"Boys," cried out crafty Benjamin,

"This boat must be, as all can see,
Turned on her other side,
Else she may never ride
Proudly again on Mexico.
'Twas sometime last year, nearer May,
That I, with father, sailed away
Down to Havana and the coast,
Where reefs are seen, and waters boast
That they can founder any boat
That tries upon their waves to float.
There this same *Pet* did calmly sail,
Not heeding half the ocean's rail,
But sped and took us to the shore
We thought we'd surely see no more."
Now made we bold
When this was told
To pull one mighty pull together,
Despite the hot and sunny weather.
"Ye ho!" cried Dexter, as he drew;
"Ye ho!" cried all the jolly crew,
So with the music and the muscle,
With all the groans and sweat and tussle,
Out came the *Pet*, showing where she
Had braved so well the angry sea.
At length we came to go,
As the red sun sank low,
And sent its rays up from the west
Where it was sinking down to rest,
For the earth was stained with a crimson light;
All the sky was scarlet and red and pink,
And the clouds were stranger than one can think,

While deepening colors threw below a shade,
Like beauty that appears as pictures fade.
Large blossoms scarcely waved along the shore,
Which shook with laughter just awhile before,
And lilies that were pure and white,
Now flushed with pleasure and delight;
And what long shadows fell behind the palms!
Soon came we 'neath a cloud of green
Which faced the sky with royal mien;
Odors rich, sweet and strong,
Fell o'er us as we moved along;
The jasmine with its pleasant smell,
Where bees and sunshine love to swell,
And oleanders that will give
Beauty and fragrance while they live;
Softly we moved, and then we sang,
First low
And slow,
Till all along
Music was echoed loud and strong.

Sunday came on, a day of rest,
Worthy to bear the name of blest,
And, in the eve, we took our way,
Some few, out toward the setting day,
Until we reached the humble church
That stood upon a rising perch
Of sand, higher than all the rest,
Clustered about, like to a nest,
With leaves and bushes overgrown,
And grasses which hda long been sown;

Rough, tumble steps led to a door
That opened out upon the floor,
And benches lay about,
Fashioned too rude and stout
To seat those used to easy-chairs.
A pulpit stretched from end to end,
And with the benches seemed to blend
In trying to be rough and plain,
Having no polish, nor a stain.
A Bible soiled, but holy still,
Lay, waiting, on the window sill,
While a few dusky people sat
Down on a round and braided mat.
Then others came, when soon along
Sat all about a mighty throng,—
All shades of black or dusky hue,
Some light, but most to Ebon true.
Something is moving through the crowd,
And now, in accents rich and loud,
A voice read out: "Please sing dis hymn,
An' cry it wid a pow'ful vim."
And so a hundred negroes sang
And shouted, as the old church rang:

"Shout, oh! shout de glory song,
Doan delay but come along,
Fer de day am 'proachin' fas'
When dis earf will hab to pass
In one dreffül, fiery mass.

"An' de moon will tu'n to blood,
An' de brooklet make a flood

Swoopin' 'bout us like de sea,
An' den, sinnah, you an' me,
Say, oh, whar, say whar'll we be?

"Oh! dis yere will be de day
Fer de bad to fall away,
An' de just will stan' apart,
Waitin' de comman' to start
Whar we goes to nebber part.

"Glory, glory! den we'll sing
All de day,
An' de wicked, lazy lout
Dat can hardly walk about,
To de debbil mus' he go
Mighty quick."

After the hymn,
When twilight dim
Took to racing
In the form of shadows weird,
Which increased the live oak's beard,
The lamps were lighted,
And the benighted
Heard loud the text, "Oh, mine is dine;"
"Mine is dine!" said the preacher,
The tall black teacher,
Who in his pulpit stood
To give his people food;
Who ever told them not to steal,
But always for their neighbors feel,
If ne'er for melons.
"An' mine is dine," he said,

"As you hab offen read,
Oh! mine is dine, dear bredderen,
Oh! dine, ah! am mine, dear sisteren.
David, de son, de king,
He knows 'bout eberyting;
An' yet he sin, dat man,
An' say de Lord do fan
De 'niquity ob mine enemy.
Oh, ah, oh, ah, ah, oh!
De Lord hab tol' us so."
And so the preacher told,
Going from hot to cold
And cold to hot,
Trying to say what he could not,
Which same thing happens oft to others
Who preach in churches, O my brothers!
Who wander from their texts so far away
They land at last into some boggy bay.
They tell of Heaven, and how we all may win it,
And preach upon it till there's nothing in it,
With Hebrew words, with dialects of Greek,
With every language but the one we speak,
And though they differ, being black or white,
They stand on common ground in needing light

CANTO II.

[*Non satis vivere, debemus bene vivere.*]

Monday morning bright and early,
Without clouds and no one surly,
We did make and leave our couches,

Get our guns and hunting pouches,
Fishing tackle and provisions,
Making manifold divisions,
For convenience and for pleasure,
In the coming days of leisure.
Bags full of bread,
Which some had said
Would more than feed
Ten times our need,
Went off on Sambo's shoulders
Like wondrous boulders,
And disappeared behind the trees,
Much as the fitful morning breeze.
Into the *Pet* they went,
While more were sent,
Blankets and sheets,
Fruits, wines, and meats,
Till Tampa stared in wild amaze,
And lengthened out her wondering gaze.
Into a store we took our way,
About the eighth hour of the day,
And there bought milk and flour,
And quantities of fruit that's sour,
Called grape fruit, and resembling much
Lemons, limes, oranges, and such;
In other words, as learned Southrons say,
Belonging to the citrus family.
Coffee we bought,
Because we thought
That it might be, out on the sea,
Better than tea,

Though of the latter we did take
Enough for several times to make
A good strong cup,
That would steam up,
And make us taste it suddenly.
At last the boat was full,
When one did pull
Small, trembling ropes,
Like certain hopes
Soon followed by
Free open sails and pleasant sky.
Now was it time to go, when a slight blow
Helped us to speed away,
Out to the restless, moving bay.
And each had bought, before he left the shore,
A wide *sombrero* in some Tampa store,
So very wide the eye grew dim
Ere it had gazed across the brim.
Hilsboro' left we in the rear,
As a small island that was near
Stretched its green body into view,
And glistened in the morning dew.
A gentle breath touched all the sea,
And rippled o'er its waters free,
While from above the sunny light
Gladdened it into liquid bright.
As on the surface fast we glide
One looked from off our small ship's side,
Wondering no doubt how deep and blue
Were the soft waves we journeyed through
He wore a wide and Southern hat,

Covering his person fair and fat;
Eyes that were large and wondrous mild;
Eyes which good-natured ere beguiled
Were his; while a full beard,
Light floating to his waist, now neared
As he bent forward and beneath
His high-crowned, wide Panama wreath.
Slightly stooped were his shoulders too,
While dark brown locks across them woo
The constant, cooling breeze
Which stirred them, as it did the trees.
A suit of dark he wore
Which often he had worn before,
And from his hat there swung about
A hempen cord of texture stout,
To keep it safe from falling out.
His pockets all were crowded full,
From household scrap to Popish bull,
With papers by the dozen,
Concerning priest and king and cousin;
Concerning house and home and cattle,
Or how to shake a baby's rattle,
All done in tidy little scrolls,
And fastened up in tissue rolls.
Much was there too about gastrology,
Not unto us a mere mythology,
But a real truth we felt each day,
As hunger proved us, on the way.
This was our right-hand man,
Who held the frying-pan,
Named for a season Dexter,

For though he didn't come from Exter,
He loved the sea,
And reveled in hydrography.
Ohio was his native State,
Where many others who are great
By chance were born,
And now adorn
That fair State's history.
It is a mystery
Why Dexter did not in his State remain,
And to the presidential chair attain,
But fate had willed it otherwise—
She has her way beneath the skies—
And soon our hero went to school,
There to learn o'er the rigid rule
Of stern theology.
But when the noise of war broke out,
Brave Dexter followed in the route;
Through all the war he fought, until
The cannon's roar and smoke were still,
When he came back
With a haversack,
And a captain's legacy.

Busy upon a piece of bread
Sat he who always sank the lead;
Brown as a nut with tropic tan
Was he, the Texas laboring man,
With common sense, but hidden deep,
And almost always fast asleep,
So unto strangers it did not appear,

But ever dawdled in the rear.
Though kind of heart, his form was coarse,
He slowly spoke in accent hoarse,
And drawled his words so very long
They ended in a dismal song.
Here sat he by an open box,
And watched it like a wily fox
Watches his game;
'Twas a sesame
That gave him privilege to eat
Another piece of tempting meat.
Tabler was this, or Fiddle-diddle,
Or both, each was a riddle,
Than try to guess 'twere better far
To leave one's fortune to a star.
Quite tall he was, his legs were short,
He used them as a last resort,
As though the will that moved the rest
Had left them, at their own request,
To follow when they felt inclined,
Or, if they wished, to stay behind.
This gave them then a paddling gait
That often made their owner late.
Now Tabler's hands were large and rough,
His arms were strong, his sinews tough;
His neck was surely long enough.
His head a shock of hair did own
That looked as if some wind had blown
It in a pyramid;
But this was only his wife's style
Of combing it, well fixed with "ile,"

A somber, solemn, cranial pile,
On which a hat did calmly rest,
Obedient to its lord's behest.
"Wal," and he swallowed with a gulp,
A wondrous piece of orange pulp,
"I reckon this yere sea is calm,
And runs as easy as a psalm.
We're movin' far out on the bay,
It will not take us half a day
Before our boat will almost be
Touching upon the old Long Quay,
That's quite a distance out at sea."
At this remark our little bark
Rushed through the water faster still,
And set to work with earnest will.
Contented Tabler, with one wayward eye,
Looked up into the cloudless sky,
But with the other gazed not there,
For his two eyes were not a pair;
One, ever faithful to his Texas home,
Looked back, wherever he might roam.

The captain's name was Benjamin,
A crafty lad was he;
He owned the boat, and manned it well;
He understood the sea.
His form was good, his face was smooth,
His moustache long and red.
He said
He came from Nebraska,
Where he was born and bred,

And told of startling deeds in which
He figured as the head.
His voice was pleasing to the ear,
And if he would he might
Speak either like a scientist,
Or as a trifler light.
So Benjamin would tell us all,
If good or bad or great or small,
About the land, the sea, the sky,
Or any fish we might descry;
About the winds, or how to sail;
About the gull, or water rail;
Here point to some outlying isle,
Or there to many a coral pile,
And thus our leisure hours beguile.

"Aye, aye, sir," said a mellow voice,
It was the helmsman—one by choice—
Who, though our equal partner in the yachting trip,
Was loth to let such an opportunity slip
As he had to learn the ways of a ship.
So the captain he
For the time made free,
To use him as his own guarantee.
Blue were his eyes, and his face was fair,
While into his heart not even a care
Had discovered the way up its golden stair.
Not a wrinkle and not a line
On his face; it was soft and fine,
Expressing its workmanship divine.
He came from a land where frost and snow

Fall from the clouds to the earth below,
And cover it all in a robe of white,
With glittering diamonds small and bright;
Where the birch and maple in gladness grow,
Where all the Canada thistles blow;
But his heart was as warm as a tropic sun
When its daily journey is not half done;
Of malice or hatred his heart had none.
But why did he not remain
In his home so far away?
Why did he seek the main
To ride through its spray?
This is what we said, but his head
He shook in a doubtful way,
Meaning—you all shall know
Why I came, another day.
I believe in the rule of a president,
And not in the reign of a king;
In my country they all believe
Just the other thing.

Last but not least came Penniman,
Who sat not far away,
In a study brown, and his form was held
In a suit of iron gray.
He looked ever ready in mood and mien
For some wild affray.
Into the war he had been, like a man, to fight;
Out of it all he came with wounds that were slight,
But it left on his cheek an impress deep,
Coming and going like shepherdless sheep.

In his every act
We could see the fact,
For he seemed to be fighting over again,
Or planning for life a silent campaign;
And over his spirits there seemed to fall
Sometimes a deep cloud like a funeral pall,
But often the sun would shine through it all.
He was a Yankee, and believed
The Constitution through,
And on his heart its very laws
In living letters grew;
And if you lauded Uncle Sam
He was at once with you.
A traveler was he o'er the globe,
A traveler whom we could not probe;
No matter what we asked or told
He never would himself unfold.
And more than this he would not tell:
In Boston, where he used to dwell,
He left his wife—a pretty belle—
Because she always dressed too well.

Down into the great wide sea
The red sun sank to rest,
Sending its soft light far and free,
Tinging the wave to its very crest;
This was the sun's farewell, for he
Was taking our daylight into the West.
And the shades of night,
In ecstatic delight,
Gathered upon the silent shore,

To worship their sweet goddess and adore.
Deeper and darker the waters grew,
For before us and o'er us
The curtains of night
Had hidden the sun and shut out its light.
"Whar are we now?" said Tabler,
As he rubbed his willful eye,
"My 'pinion is we're movin'
Jes' as fast as we can fly,
And I 'speck we're goin' outwards
Like a Neptune on the sea;
Though I'm not afraid of water,
I think now perhaps we'd orter
Betake ourselves to land,
But whar and how to git thar
I do not understand.
Accordin' to my own idee
I reckon that it's time for tea,
For one poor meal a day can't keep
A man alive unless he's sleep."
"All right, then, general," cried the captain quick,
"You are a daisy and a brick;
Steady the helm;
Just see that all is right,
And I will see you into port before the moon is bright."
"Aye, aye, sir, your commands I hear,
Just shift the sails and I will steer."
So in we came between two islands dark,
Which stood like guards on either side our bark,
While through the trees we caught the shimmering light
Of a now rising moon so pale and white.

Higher and higher fair Luna pushed her way
Into the gladdened sky;
Larger and larger grew the ray,
Till by and by
It covered all the heaven with light—
And such, in Florida, is night.
Up to the very shore we took our *Pet*,
And landed without getting wet.
Meanwhile the captain fixed the sails,
Dipped out the water with the pails,
Spread up the canopy—a sheet,
And made it look so nice and neat,
A very little home complete.
"Out with provisions, we shall have a fire
That will with heartiness inspire
Us all and each to one desire,
And this to make a fragrant cup
Of coffee strong, and drink it up."
One took some boxes from the bark,
Another kindled with a spark
Upon the sand, a cheery fire,
That soon created havoc dire
Among the branches that were brought,
Of mangrove roots and gnarled oak knot,
With which the shore was strewn about—
An army for the sea to rout.
Upon the hard white beach we sat;
No Persian prince had better mat
In all his palace than was that.
Now in the frying-pan there went
Some savory meat, of which the scent

And kindly flavor almost made
It very subject to a raid.
"Have patience, Tabler, do not fret;
The supper is not ready yet;
It will be, soon as we can get
The bacon fried, the coffee boiled,
The wild meat done and nicely broiled.
We're getting things upon the table,
And just the minute we are able
We shall sit down to such a feast
As ne'er was served to man or beast."
So spake the cook; the kettle in assent
Hummed o'er that song that makes all men content,
And seemed in making good cheer all intent.
"This makes me think," said Penniman,
As he stirred up the frying-pan,
That sputtered loud as such things can,
"This makes me think of islands of the sea,
Such islands as, for instance, Hawaii,
Where, covered with tall palms as here there be,
The natives do, some tranquil night,
Disport themselves in rare delight,
Making, as we have made, a fire upon the beach,
But leaving, as we shall not leave, some bones to bleach—
At any rate I hope we may not leave our own,
Or any which the ghost of man could own."

Round the fire now all were seated,
Each one served and no one cheated;
First came bread and then came butter,
Ham and eggs—with noisy splutter—

Hard-tack biscuits soaked in water;
A broiled goose, 'twas Dexter shot her
With his little short revolver.
In the coffee found we pleasure,
And we drank our cup's full measure;
Thus we drank in days of leisure.
Then the dishes cleared away,
By the fire we snugly lay,
Planning for another day.
Into the air bright sparks were kindled,
Upward they went until they dwindled,
Dwindled, dwindled, dwindled, and dwindled,
Falling at last to earth in a cinder,
Only a blackened, crisped-up tinder.
How like some men, and we thought as we wondered,
Who, starting right, have afterwards blundered,
And fallen to earth as anathemas thundered,
Or like some others who in honor have started,
Meeting with insult from which they have smarted,
Lost all their courage—while glory departed.

THE CAPTAIN'S STORY.

"Listen, my comrades, while I tell,"
  Cried Benjamin, our captain gay,
"And give attention, if your thoughts
  Are not employed another way.

"For as you sit around the fire,
  And look each other in the face,
Thinking about the homes you left,
  Your wondrous change of scene and place,

"It may be well to think upon
Things that transpired long years ago,
From the far North, and up the coast,
Down to the Everglades below.

"Through all the land blood-guilty Spain,
Discovering Florida, had made,
Upon the tribes who owned it all,
Many a wrong and shameful raid.

"Boasting of a religion which,
They held, from God and truth came down,
They with it hid their lawless deeds,
And feared not either curse or frown.

"Well known to history and the world
Are all the wicked acts of Spain,
And the revenge of angry wrath
Which quickly followed in their train.

"If noble Ponce de Leon found
The holy waters that he sought,
His followers, in the after years,
The bitter streams of Marah brought.

"They lifted high their standard here,
Not asking even right to come,
And treated all the wondering tribes
As heartless creatures, blind and dumb.

"While carnage reigned, and blood was shed
Out to this islet lone, there came
A solitary monk, who sought
The holy joy of peace—not fame.

"It was a maiden, and her form
Was wrapped in deep and safe disguise;
Her locks, though short, were dark and soft,
And heaven's blue shone in her eyes.

"Fame had she left on that far shore
To which she never would return;
In her white bosom, deep, there lay
The spark of what had ceased to burn,—

"A mighty love that once had filled
The very soul of her who now
Was wearing, with a patient grace,
Its stinging thorns upon her brow.

"Valencia and Alcoy,
Castellon of the mighty plain—
To all she bade a sad adieu
And vowed she ne'er would see again.

"She entered in her forest home,
With priestly gown and mournful hood;
No one was there to help her build
Her house of thatch and rustic wood.

"For food she caught the rabbit shy,
And took the tender cabbage palm;
But many hours she whiled away
In penance and in prayerful psalm.

"The years sped by, but still this monk
E'er faithful to her island was;
In other lands new kings were made,
And ruled with ever-changing laws.

"Here she became a friend to all,
The Indians flocked from far around
To ask for medicine, and have
Their wounds and painful lesions bound.

"The pale-face daughter, was she called,
Whom the Great Spirit loved so well,
But whence she came or how she lived
Not e'en the Indian could tell.

"She gave the islands near her own
The very names this day they bear,
And drew upon a parchment white,
In careful writing, fine and fair,

"A map of her environs each,
With islets dotted here and there,
Their rivers and their lakes and bays,
Put down with all a woman's care.

"Just north of us is Egmont's Key,
Covered with mangrove trees and palm;
There Esperitu Santo, where
The sailors find it ever calm.

"She named sweet Sara Sota Bay,
Whose waters wash so many isles,
And all the narrow straits where pass
The rushing waters in their wiles.

"'Tis said she spoke the Indian tongues,
And taught the tribes deep in the Word;
While Christian peace came down to those
Who listened and who gladly heard.

"And thus her influence did spread
Until it reached o'er all the land,
Till Tlathopopkahatchee came
To tribute pay with his own hand.

"Name all your lakes, the priestess said,
After your good men as they die,
So they may have a record here,
As well as records up on high.

"And so the chief went gladly back
And named his own possessions all,
The names of which we now may know
If yet we may not each recall.

"Thonolosassa, for a lake;
With la Koochee, Hickpochee;
Choconicla, Ocklawaha
And old Olia kon'konhee.

"Long after, when the chief returned,
The maid was on the isle no more;
Silence was round—the hamlet stood
Deep hid with vines and clustered o'er.

"Loud called the chief, no answer came,
The forest echoed back the sound,
While its reverberations rolled
On through the islands far around.

"As Tlathopopkahatchee took
His homeward way, by chance he found,
Well hidden under mossy oaks
In the deep wood, a lonely mound;

"And, bending o'er the wooden slab,
He read the name of her who taught
Him how to read; who left those truths
Nor gold nor treasure could have bought.

"Her name was Anna Mária,
The same this pleasant island bears;
Her grave is here, not far away;
Let him disturb her rest who dares.

"From Nassau to Monroe and Dade,
Where'er an Indian you see,
Speak only this poor maiden's name,
And he will to you friendly be.

"Her history all is known to them,
Unknown to us. Her plighted love
Is oft the theme for Indian tales,
And, speaking, they will point above.

"Tis growing late, you must not wait;
I've told you quite enough to-night,
And though the moon is shining bright,
She may before long take her flight,
And leave us all in such a plight,
Out of the boat without a light."
"A word before we go,"
Said Penniman the wise,
"Where shall we travel to when next
The sun does o'er our visage rise?"
'To-morrow of to-morrow will
Take the best care I think;
Let Nature for itself look out,

So said the bobolink,"
And so said Tabler, with a sleepy bow
As wisely as his tongue knew how.
Dexter lay stretched out on the sand,
His head upon a log,
An easy pillow, one by which
The rest were kept agog,
To know if all this mist of sleep
Were nothing but a fog.
Often the eyes of one would blink,
And sometimes on his breast would sink
His weary head,
While everybody thought 'twas time
For all to go to bed.

So now into our boat we went,
With hearts brimful of sweet content,
While under the fair firmament
The blankets were spread,
Our prayers were all said,
We jumped into bed
And covered our head.

VOICES.

Good-night, good-night,
Sweet people all,
The darkness deep begins to fall;
Sleep fast and do not wake till morn,
When Gabriel blows his merry horn,
And daylight shall again be born.
Fairies then again shall flee

Back into the moving sea.
Sleep on then all till morning light,
Good-night, good-night, good-night, good-night.

CANTO III.

The night had gone,
A rising dawn
Fell softly over land and sea;
While one awoke,
And silence broke
By calling out vehemently:
"Wake up! wake up! the sun is high,
We must be moving by and by,
And ere we sail out from the shore,
We should our beauteous isle explore."
Breakfast well over, down a path
Now covered with an aftermath,
We slowly moved with careful eye
So game or relics we should spy,
Through varied woods of oak and balm,
Of bay tree and of cabbage palm,
As over all a floor of green was spread,
On which might fairy princes tread
When they held merry matins overhead.
Across the path many a tree clasped hands,
Vowing eternal friendship; while with bands
Of bamboo and of grape their oath's demands
Sacred were made.
More narrow grew the winding way,
And 'neath the tangled vines that lay

At its far end stretched all around,
Anna Maria's grave we found.
The wooden slab was there no more,
A simple cross of oak instead,
While underneath her name was read—
And not a single word we said.
Tabler did now the silence break,
And from his reverie awake;
As tears stood in one pensive eye,
He lifted up his head on high
To show the other was not dry.
With great surprise, we all began
To wonder how our Texas-man
Had now discovered cause for grief,
And called these tears to his relief.
"Waal," said he as he wiped his eyes
And brushed his bedimmed vision clear,
"I will declar', I shed a tear,
Which doesn't happen onc't a year,
And why it has don't now appear.
This ain't no time to make excuse,
And 'twouldn't be no kind of use,
For you can see it aint my style
To be a cryin' like a chile.
For when I lets my feelin's out,
'Tis cause they're pushed by suthin' stout,
That won't recede or turn about;
Jes' as them waves swells on the sea,
And rush and heave toward you and me;
Jes' as the boomin' hurricane
Flies swoopin' o'er the level plain;

Jes' as clouds comes into the sky
And brings the rain-drops, by and by;
Jes' so them ere tears starts to fall,
And why I cannot tell at all.
I specks there's suthin' moves the whole,
That makes the water toss and roll,
That tells the wind blow strong and loud,
And presses rain-drops from the cloud.
So then my fren's there suthin' here
That axed my fountain for a tear."
"I'm glad your fountain is not dry,"
Said Penniman, in slow reply,
"For such things empty often are
In men who travel long and far,
Especially if they go West
And in dry land their means invest.
They find then, but, alas! too late,
They need their tears to irrigate;
No other water far or near
Falls on their acres—save a tear.
Oft too their wives will help to shed—
Poor women—from an aching head,
Tears—till their eyes are swollen red.
'Tis a good sign, my friend, that you
Have well preserved some youthful dew,
For had you wept o'er Texas land
And watered Matagorda sand,
Your springing well, with hollow sound,
Would at your earnest call resound."
"Thanks, mister, you are very kind;
I'll tell you, if you do not mind,

That not a drop is left behind.
My Texas ranch wan't worth a tear,
If it did cost me mighty dear—
But now I specks we better steer."
Nearly the day we spent—a long, bright day,
Whose gleams were moving to the west away;
Much had we seen and gathered from the isle,
Much to remember and our thoughts beguile,
When, in the after years—some future time—
We came in memory to this sunny clime.
But shadows, like grim ghosts on hands and knees,
Crept hovering ever toward the mossy trees,
Stole up their trunks, and, in a spreading cloud,
Hung down a floating drapery of shroud.
Swift from the flowers, where all day long they fed,
The humming bees in anxious hurry sped;
Night birds came out, and owl, with hoot and screech,
Hysteric laughter made from oak and beech;
Like hay-field music was the locusts' song,
That sounded from the tree-tops all along.
Then up from the island there suddenly rose
A thunder of groanings and puffings and blows,
Like a very earthquake under one's nose.
Ho! for the frogs their band was now playing,
Listen! the leader his notes is conveying.
Oh! what a concert we had without paying!
For out of the swamp a thousand frogs sang,
Both large ones and small ones with guttural twang:
"We're a gang, a gang, we're a noisy gang."
Better by far than many a choir,
That, seated up somewhere under some spire,

Are never contented but looking up higher;
Playing and singing according to note,
Very much too by rule and by rote,
Taking a license and trying to float
Each his own voice through the atmosphere thick,
Bass sounding deep like the fall of a brick,
Tenor falsetto, and fearfully quick—
Save me, I pray, for the thought makes me sick.

Though every ray of light had gone,
And night its heavy curtains drawn,
We stood and listened to each charming sound,
Which made sweet music through the forest round.
"But let us go," at length one of us said,
"Or we may not till morning find our bed.
The way is long and narrow—if the isle be small,
'Tis easy to be lost here after all,
And for a night in this dark wilderness
I am not longing, I confess."
We started then in a jolly trot,
And our feet flew fast, for we surely thought
Of a supperless night and an empty cot,
Of snakes and of panthers, of scorpions too.
Oh, what in the world should we ever do?
At last came we to a wonderful end,
Where the path and forest seemed to blend,
And into a mystery of limbs extend.
There were limbs above and limbs down below,
And limbs where they never ought to grow,
For they crossed and twisted in close embrace—
'Twas a very mysterious sort of place.
No matches had we in our marvelous luck;

In the jungle and darkness we firmly were stuck;
And we scrambled through thicket, o'er bramble and bush,
With effort determined, with pull and with push.
"Now, boys," cried out Dexter, "in our first camisade
We must keep well together, or out of the raid
Someone will be lost, I am now much afraid.
There's no telling what things lie under these branches,
As ugly and fierce as the thirsty Comanches;
For I think this strange place with beasts is infested,
And the trees feel like mangroves long grown unmolested."
"Hello, thar! hello, thar! I say thar *hello!*"
Was a sound that came up from some puddle below;
"I'm down on my back and fast in the mud,"
So Tabler exclaimed as he fell with a thud.
"We are coming," we shouted, "but where do you lie,"
And the thought came upon us, if Tabler should die
Before we his shape in the darkness can spy.
All the while he was sitting and scraping his clothes,
For Tabler was quick, as this incident shows.
"Are you up?" and we laughed, restraining our mirth,
"Are you out of the mud and up from the earth?"
But in process of cleaning ne'er Tabler would deign
To answer our questions—so asked we in vain.

Now came the rain-drops pattering loud,
New offspring of some pregnant cloud,
On shrub it fell, on leaf, and frond,
Or back into the jealous pond,
Which, full and almost flowing o'er,
Begs from the clouds for more and more.
Another cloud, in strange delight,

Scatters Jove's bolts throughout the night,
Paling the heavens into fright,
While angry thunder's pealing roar
Rolls and resounds along the shore—
'Twas a Florida storm and nothing more..
But we saw through the flash and the blaze
We had stumbled along to a mangrove maze,
And were lost in the midst of its intricate ways.
Up high on a limb
Sat the form of him
Whose chances for drying were wofully slim;
And he looked in the light
Like a goblin sprite
Who might be around upon such a night.
Soaking and wet,
So far from the *Pet*,
By light—all electric—we huddled together,
A lot of poor travelers, deep under the weather;
And clustered about round the trunk of a tree,
Adown which were running the waters so free,
We shivered and wished we were having our tea.
Down came the rain, and boom went the thunder,
Crash fell a tree, with its limbs split asunder,
And the swamp shuddered in turn, and no wonder!
While the storm roared and never relented,
Raging and groaning like manhood demented,
Worse than King Lear when he cried and lamented.
We slept, I suppose,
For through somebody's nose
Came a story of woes.
Once or twice Dexter woke,

And in dream voice he spoke,
For he thought we were sailing
With high winds prevailing;
As he asked who was bailing
We gave him a poke,
And so in a trice thus ended the joke.

At last fair Aurora, with glistening eye,
Sent a glimmer of daybreak athwart thro' the sky,
While we moved with the shadows and out of the marsh,
Resenting our treatment as cruel and harsh.
Chilly and wet and shivering too,
Moved our sad and hungry crew,
As the mocking gay curlew,
Shrieking out, " How do you do? "
High above our bowed heads, flew.
Upon the beach quite unabashed
Great waves in restless motion dashed,
And pushed and tumbled o'er and o'er,
With noise incessant and with roar,
While in the east the morning sun
Called for his steed, that had begun
To fret and worry, wondering why
They were not riding through the sky.
With royal mien fair Helios took
His chariot seat, as shades forsook
His path, and hid in some recess
Of sombrous cloud or wilderness;
Glanced from the wheels rays warm and bright,
And soon sent out the dark of night.
All clouds were gone, an open sky

Stretched o'er our heads so grand and high—
We only wished our clothes were dry.
Wishes we knew would not avail,
Actions alone could aught prevail,
And so with pluck quite wondrous, we
Made a good fire to steep our tea,
And in one hour were out at sea.
Spent was the anger of the wind,
And though it blew its touch was kind;
It filled the sail and gave us speed,
Then passed along, not giving heed
To what the grumbling ocean said,
Though from its sleep and quiet bed,
The night before, the wind had pitched
The great sea out, almost bewitched;
But soon it woke, and white with rage
Demanded fierce a war to wage,
Fumed, roared, and called upon the rain
To aid the cause, nor called in vain.
Thus had he felt through all the night
The wrestlings of that dreadful fight.
But now the wind of a forgiving mind
Had left its wrath in some deep cave behind,
And touched the sea, now here and there,
With quite a vain and jaunty air.
Deep as the ocean is, its wrath was deep,
It would not hear of rest or sleep,
But long did a resentful spirit keep.
Wave after wave our little *Pet*
With lightsome bound all eager met,
Making a feather of the load

It bore so bravely as we rode.
"Now, boys," said Benjamin, "to-day
I think some fish will be at play
Or work, it matters not if we
Can only view them well, and see.
Southeast we sail out toward some islands small,
And though they be not named I know them all.
Beauties they are, small gems of lovely green,
Covered with palms of graceful mien,
And quite surrounded by a snow-white beach
That has upon it shells for Sol to bleach.
These isles would be the very soul's delight
Of some poor monk or anchorite,
Or one who, tired of vain applause,
Has left the world to study Nature's laws.
But look here, lads, there goes a school
Of tempting mullet: see them fool
About the boat; I wish we might
Have a good meal out of the sight.
They all are fat and taste right smart
To any man who eats a part.
See! there's a skipper riding fast,
His tail the rudder, and himself the mast!"
All day, to some sight entertained,
We viewed and each in wisdom gained;
Saw porpoise ploughing through the wave,
Their large, mild eyes so sad and grave,
Asking for food we quickly gave;
And flying fish with finny wings—
Such strange, eccentric little things!
And sharks whose ugly dorsal fin

Cropped out like some vain-glorious sin
That e'er is out, and ne'er will in;
And water-snakes; and turtles large
That moved along like some vast barge
With ponderous load and heavy charge.
Ah! what a host of herrings small;
Of things that were not fish at all,
Of sailing shells, anemones,
And other things brought by the breeze,
Till night drew on and found us where
We could approach without a care
Near to the mainland, whose wide shore
Was strewn with coral, shells, and ore.
Back was a forest, dense and deep,
In which scarce daylight dared to peep,
But looked at dusk, like some abattis made
To guard a fortress or resist a raid.
After our supper, after night fell down,
As each one lay wrapped in a study brown,
There rose from out the sea a little arc,
A tiny speck of white, a silver bark,
A pretty sight to see just after dark.
But soon it turned to be a crescent fair,
Such as may oft be seen 'most anywhere.
Slowly the orb rose upward, as a beam,
Glanced down to meet the up-reflected gleam,
From which embrace sprang offspring clear and bright—
A golden line—that trembling path of light
In which the fairies travel after night.
They come in thousands thro' the moonlit ray,
Down to our earth, but ne'er forget do they,

When Morning's path is made, to go away—
Of this was thinking Dexter as he lay.
"Now," said he to the rest, "if you desire,
I with a tale will you sweet thoughts inspire,
And tell you what I read long years ago,
If true or not, I say I do not know.
Not far from here, for so the legends say,
On an indented island in our bay,
Was treasure hid by some wild buccaneer—
No date is given to us, and no year—
Before old Chronos reigned it was, I fear;
So prick your ears to what I now shall tell,
And wake you up, and listen well.

VIOLA'S CHARM.

"'Tis told that centuries ago
There lived in Spain a lady rich,
And whoe'er did her beauty know
Felt its deep power their souls bewitch.

"Not only wealth in house and gold,
But wealth in form had she as well;
What charms were hers, though often told,
'Twas said no human tongue could tell.

"Among a score of suitors, there
Were only two the maid received,
And of the two she most did care
For bold Andrino, all believed.

"Though Don Fernando often came
And often saw the lady, too,

The question was to win the dame
Who would, and which the damsel woo.

"True 'twas, Viola loved but one
Of the gay courtiers who did pay
Their kind attentions, now begun
And growing bolder day by day.

"And he, Fernando was, a youth
To whom she gave her heart and hand,
But whom in combat, for a truth,
Could not his rival well withstand.

"Viola feared Andrino's rage
No less than his more steady blade;
'But time his passion will assuage,'
Declared the eager, loving maid!

"Yet as time sped and months flew by,
The knight his love told ever on,
Nor wearied he; but well did ply
His suit till eve from early dawn.

"One balmy day Viola felt
She could not wait much longer now,
And told Fernando, as he knelt,
Of her own feelings deep, and how

"She hoped and waited, trusting he,
Fernando's rival, soon would cease
To seek or love her, so that she
Could marry her true love in peace.

"But now to longer wait were vain:
She had a plan she would unfold;
And though the thought did give her pain,
'Twas needful that it soon be told.

"And ere she told, her lover made
A promise of deep secrecy,
Till all their plans matured as laid
Had worked out their conspiracy.

"'In that far country of the West,'
The guilty maiden thus began,
'Is hidden treasure—a bequest—
Unknown since years to any man.

"''Tis buried in some obscure isle;
The will lies hidden with the gold,
And grants to him the precious pile
Who seeks and finds it in the mould.

"'Placed there it was by father's sire,
Panfilo de Narvaez, brave,
Whose valiant deeds do yet inspire
To works of good and acts that save.

"'He to my father left a charm
By which the island might be found,
As e'en the spot where strength of arm
Must seek the treasure underground.

"'This charm has lain in disregard,
And is a useless thing to me;
So now, Fernando, do thou guard
It as my offering to thee.

"'For it will give thee, more than gold,
Possession of my face and form;
Of graces which shall yet unfold
From out a bosom true and warm.

"'And I will Don Andrino tell
Of this my plan—that thou and he
To our dear Spain bid short farewell,
And sail across the mighty sea.

"'Find in our country far away
(What thou hast aid to easy find),
And, coming back that very day,
Viola claim with tranquil mind.

"'Go, tell your rival that I will
He come with thee to-morrow eve,
Where, in our garden cool and still,
I may his mind and ours relieve.'

"Thus spoke the damsel as she left
In Don Fernando's hand the charm
Which he, with senses nigh bereft,
Closed down upon in quick alarm.

"A craven fear filled all his soul,
And, trembling now in every limb,
He knew guilt, like some midnight ghoul,
Was surely creeping over him.

"The morrow came; then twilight soft,
That fell upon a garden spot
Where wooing branches high aloft
Seemed with celestial music fraught.

"And on a rustic seat below
Sat Viola with both her knights,
To whom in accents false and low
She thus a wicked speech indites:

"'List, noble lovers, you have sought
My heart and hand so long and well,
I cannot say I love you not;
Which love the best, I cannot tell.

"'So to your ears I will disclose
A plan to set all matters right,
And spare us each such cruel words
As spring from wrath and jealous fight.

"'There is in our new land afar,
On some small island of the sea,
Hidden great wealth; what may debar
You, lords, from searching it for me?

"'To him who finds the gift shall be
The gold he found, and I will give
Him all he ever asks of me;
Be all his own while he shall live.

"'For this will show which best deserves
The love of her, who, speaking now,
Much loves you both, and yet reserves
The most for him with crownéd brow.

"'Who with success and lasting fame
Comes to receive the greater meed,
That valiant strength and wisdom claim;
Which will be worthy crown indeed.

"'Now, promise, knights, give me your word
That by this search you will abide,
And each by oath upon his sword
Show how you win or lose a bride.'

"Then these two knights did gladly kneel
Before that autocratic maid,
And promise ne'er to clash their steel,
But that her will would be obeyed.

"'As many other fools have done
Before these two and after them,—
With promises as rash—like one
I do remember well—a-hem!

"A man in love sees by the moon,
His daylight wrapped in shadow lies;
Judgment trips off on some monsoon,
That blows his reason to the skies.

"'Tis sad but true that men do lose
The very time when most they need
The wits they had, then quite refuse
To let the wits of others lead,

"But swear they know their own affairs
Better than saner men would know.
I say, who fall in Cupid's snares
'Tis ever best to let them go.

"'And,' said the damsel, 'one thing yet
To both I give this much advice:
Do not return here till you get
The gain or loss, at any price.

"'Go! and God bless you in your task;
Don Carlo's ship to-morrow sails;
If you would from me something ask,
Ask quickly, then; for night prevails.

"'No answer! well, I take it then
You both brave lords are satisfied.
Farewell! and I may meet you when
One of you knights shall claim his bride.'

"Two months had gone; one sunny day,
With soft, warm winds and smiling skies,
A weary ship slow on its way
Into a tropic harbor hies.

"Its sails were tattered well, and torn;
A Spanish flag hung in the breeze,
Showing dim colors sadly worn,
And harshly treated by the seas.

"A motley crew stood on the deck
Of seamen rough and buckled knight,
All gazing at a distant speck
That danced and trembled in their sight.

"But nearer came they, till it grew
Into an oval form of green,
With palm trees tall from which there flew
Gay birds with necks of sparkling sheen.

"Gulls, white and brown, and speckled o'er,
Rose, now alarmed, with flapping wing;
While round it all a circling shore
Inclosed it like some wizard's ring.

"'Look, noble youths,' the captain said;
'To this fair land our fathers came,
And to its shores were hither led
By love of honor, and of fame.

"'I trust that you have worthy aims
And come here to perpetuate,
By valiant deeds, your honored names,
As some have done who now are great.

"'Pardon me if I seem too bold;
Know that I have your good at heart,
For you are young, while I am old;
So tell me truly as we part,

"'If trouble bring ye here alone
Out to this country wild and new,
To seek in wrath—calm reason flown—
Revenge which ye must surely rue.

"'Ne'er gave it peace to any man;
'Twill not atone for any sin;
It doth the flame of anger fan
And drive its pain but deeper in.'

"'Well, we believe thee, honest friend;'
And, listening, thus Don Carlos heard,
Our two knights make suave amend
For silent mood and sullen word.

"'But we come not with evil mind,
Nor do we wish each other ill;
For both here come to search and find
A long and nigh forgotten will.

"'Thinking of this, forgotten were
Things more apparent and more near
Since what we search is but for her—
We shall not quarrel; do not fear.'

"Now running here and running there,
With stern command and startling shout,
Dark-visaged sailors everywhere
Great ropes and cordage swung about.

"Till suddenly the anchor dropped,
And sank into the shallow tide;
As quick the ponderous vessel stopped
And tossed the waters from its side.

"'Sir knights, adieu! I leave you each
To go your way, where'er that be,
While I and my poor ship do reach
Some trading islands south of me.

"'Jupiter inlet this we call;
A few kind friends live just within,
Where open hearts, though hamlet small,
Will glad receive their blood and kin.'

"And so the captain bade adieu
To our lone lords, who quickly went
Into the forest, and from view
In search of house and dwelling bent.

"Down through a path they found their way,
Past cherry, oak, and walnut tree;
Past iron-wood and silver bay,
And dogwood and mahogany.

"Through palm, and hickory red and white;
By poplar, cypress, gum, and ash;
Magnolias whose blossoms might
The Amazon's fair flowers abash.

"As over all the clinging vine
With mild persuasion, binding still,
The branches which it did entwine,
Ruled over with an iron will.

"'Ah!' thought Andrino, 'what has He,
Our Lord, kept back from out his store,
That ever and anon should we
Be asking yet for more and more?

"'Now, as I walk my heart expands,
I feel my own inanity;
And realize that my demands
Are oft but prayers of vanity.

"'At times I ask I know not what,
And grow content by less and less,
As in my greed I have forgot
The very blessings I possess.'

"At last they reach a garden small,
In which a homely cottage stood,
Where orange grew and plantain tall,
And many other kinds of wood.

"Agavés straight and yucca blades,
Mimosas held in quivering green;
And flowers, sweet in many shades,
From pink and blue to mazarine.

" Within a latticed portico,
Up which trailed graceful clematis,
Stretched in a hammock snug and low
Swung there a pretty little miss

" None else there seemed about but her,
And she asleep was, fast and sound;
So watched the knights but did not stir,
For much they were in wonder bound.

" A girl it was whose fairy shape
Lay wrapped in careless robes of white;
Her tresses like a sable cape
Fell o'er her shoulders soft and light.

" Down by her side a romance lay,
Forgotten quite, or in some dream
Told over in a different way,
With grander plot and larger scheme.

" A smile was on her face, her breast
In trembling motion rose and fell;
'Ah! maiden of thy snowy nest
The mystery what tongue can tell?'

" Thus thought Andrino as he stood,
And drank the wondrous beauty in:
'Oh! in such heavenly shapes how could
There ever creep the shame of sin?

" 'Therein lie hidden, strong and deep,
Feelings that will in after years
Thy heart and soul and body keep,
In sure reserve for joy or tears.'

"Now with a start the damsel woke—
Some power mesmeric warned her sense—
And, flushing crimson, quickly spoke
With air of righteous insolence:

"'What business have ye two to be—
Strangers withal and here unknown—
Gazing like idiots to see
A maiden sleeping and alone?'

"'Pardon, sweet maid, and do forgive'—
Andrino spoke in pleasing tone—
'Us knights who truly would not give
Thee cause for anger had we known

"'The way to go in this great wood,
Or where else might we shelter find,
From Spain came we, our kinship should
Take fear of danger from thy mind.'

"'I ask thee pardon, noble knight,
For my impetuosity;
But greatly startled, in my fright
Uttered I words too thoughtlessly.

"'Take seats within, and I will go
To seek my parents in the dell
Where they have gone, for now I know
They will receive thee wondrous well.'

"'Her glance and word are but for thee,'
Said Don Fernando with a sneer,
As down the garden light and free
The maiden's form did disappear.

" 'She smiles upon the handsome one
And looks not at the lesser light,
But we shall see when we have done
Which comes out victor in the fight.'

" 'What angry devil has within
Thee once more broken bolt and bar,
And, like some guilty, jealous sin,
Sounded his tocsin from afar?

" 'Know that I will not quarrel now,
Nor e'er again; so hold thy tongue,
And if by chance upon thy brow
The wreath of victory should be flung,

" 'I shall not trouble thee, nor show
My shadow 'twixt thee and thy light;
But act so all the world may know
How keeps his oath a worthy knight.

" 'Though thou who art a coward born,'
Kept on Andrino, in his rage,
'I love thee not and with thee scorn
To ever in a feud engage.

" 'If thou dost gain the treasure rich,
And win Viola's hand as well,
'Twill be I know by aid of witch
Or some enchantment dark from hell.'

"Quick as a flash, Fernando took
His sword and plunged it in the breast
Of him who spoke, and then betook
Himself of other home in quest.

"The wounded lord lay on the floor,
Unconscious and of ghastly hue,
As maid and parent near the door
With quickening pace all eager drew.

"Not waiting questions vain to ask,
They took the youth and gently bound—
The maiden aiding in their task—
With healing salve, his bleeding wound.

"And so the daughter nursed him on,
From day to day and week to week,
Till many days and weeks were gone,
And color touched again his cheek.

"To his kind friends Andrino told
Oft of his search, now long delayed;
About the will and all its gold,
Nor did forget the Spanish maid.

"But as he spoke of her, the eyes
Of his young nurse would flash and flame,
Her head bend low, like one who tries
To hide from view a modest shame.

"And as he gazed upon the face,
Many a time he thought how pure,
And even heavenly, was the grace
Which he who won her would secure.

"He loved her, though he knew it not,
Far better than the faithless child
Who by deceptive practice brought
Him to this tropic land so wild.

"And she loved him, and knew it well,
With all a maiden's burning zeal,
Which trembling hand and blushes tell,
And which no maid can e'er conceal.

"Now, every day Andrino grew
Better, and strength came to his arm,
While round his heart love's halo threw
Its cheerful radiance soft and warm,

"Till after while he realized
Without this love he could not live;
And far above mere treasure prized
What would him sweeter comfort give.

"One morning then, before the sun
Poured its rich rays upon the earth,
While yet the skies were gray and dun,
And no fires kindled on the hearth,

"Andrino lay in wakeful mood,
Thinking of what he soon should do;
How, ere he left that shady wood
He must his faithful guardian woo.

"'Already I believe her heart
Is won by mine, as mine by hers,
While each to each does love impart,
Though open sufferance each defers.

"'I can no longer rest in doubt,
Since doubt no longer rests with me,
But I will quickly set about
And make my declaration free.

"'As for the one I left in Spain,
No more I love her, nor her gold,
And I will never search again
For paltry treasure in the mould,

"'Since I have found far better worth
Than such a love as honor gains,
Or prosperous searching round the earth
O'er mountain, forests, hills, or plains.'

"In musings similar, the maid
Oft in her chamber, after dark,
Launched on her sea, yet half afraid,
Fond longings in Hope's fragile bark;

"And feared she knew not what might turn
That bark upon some hidden rock,
For pleasant wind and wave to spurn,
And for an angry sea to mock.

"Yet had she found a mystic charm,
E'en on the day Fernando gave
To his brave comrade that deep harm
Which almost brought him to his grave.

"For as he took his sword, there fell
Out of his pocket to the ground
Viola's charm, that proved so well
Exacting payment for the wound.

"And in a letter wrapped about
The magic thing, Viola gave
As best she knew the proper route,
That toil she might her lover save.

"This read the maiden Felisa,
Nor understood its import till
She heard the tale of Viola,—
Of hidden wealth and mouldy will.

"Then to her senses, like a flash
Of lightning from some passing cloud,
Came the full meaning of the rash
And treacherous act; and like a shroud

"It folded her pure heart all up,
And bound it with a deep regret;
She thought 'twould be a bitter cup
For her dear noble friend, and yet,

"Perhaps, if but he knew, he might
Love her as she did him, and be
Her own, as she would his, delight.
'And shall I show him this?' said she,

"'This charm and letter? No, he must,
If love me ever, love me now,
Before I break the wreath of trust
Placed by Viola on his brow.'"

And here stopped Dexter in his tale,
As though his heart and tongue did fail
To more relate;
For Luna now had hidden deep
Her laughing face and gone to sleep;
Nor would she longer vigils keep,
But called it late.
While echoes all the shore along

Caught Tabler snoring loud and strong,
And did his nasal notes prolong.
"I think 'tis growing late, my friends,
And for my tale will make amends
By ending for the night,"
Said Dexter, as he fixed his couch,
And twisted round his hunting pouch
From left to right.
"No, no," cried his companions all;
"It is not very late at all;
And ere we close our eyes,
We wish to hear of Viola,
But most if gentle Felisa
Did win her noble prize.
No matter if our Tabler snores,
No doubt his troubled spirit soars
Into Elysian skies."
"But don't stay thar," cried Tabler quick,
"My wife she says I never stick
In any place;
As though a man were like a brick
To be stuck down with mortar thick,
Or like some dangerous lunatic,
I do declar
'Tis fit to make a parson swar.
But, frien', tell on that purty tale
Of which I did the sense inhale
A while ago.
I think we left off whar them knights
Was havin' out their jealous spites.
I want to know

How Don Fandrino did behave,
For he was nothing but a knave
And sure deserved a fiddler's grave."
"Without more parley and more fuss,
Since you all seem unanimous
In asking for my story,
I will tell how it came to pass
Our noble lord and his sweet lass
United were by holy mass
In matrimonial tie;
So listen, friends, a little more;
Not long it will be now before
The end we spy."

"Andrino, fretting at the fate
That kept him prisoner so long,
More restless grew, and could not wait
Till he was really well and strong;

"But strength enough he had to make
His wishes known to maid and sire,
Which, well received, did new awake
Felisa's love and pure desire.

"She felt now that her secret might
Be told Andrino, without fear;
Indeed, thought she, it is but right
That he the monstrous plot should hear.

And so she told him, as his cheek
Grew red and white alternately,
And his poor tongue refused to speak,
Or muttered incoherently.

"'Couldst thou then love the lass so well?'
The damsel at his side did ask,
'Or dost thou some regret the spell
That takes thee from thy weary task?'

"'In error art thou, gentle maid,'
The lord made answer, as he pressed
Her clinging hand, and softly laid
A throbbing head upon his breast,

"'Before I heard this, thou dost know
I asked thee, love, to be my bride;
Far better than all else below
I love thee, and all things beside.

"'But shocked I felt to hear of her,
Whom I believed was true and kind,
As one who could so sadly err
And plot and plan with evil mind.

"'And, oh! I thank the Lord that he
Did send me to this wonder-land,
To find my treasure all in thee;
A mighty wealth of heart and hand.

"'Aye, thankful that I have escaped
Seeking to find what such a youth,
Whose paths in windings dark are shaped,
Would soon have easy found, forsooth.

"'But now, my love, when may we wed?
The earth is fair, and summer skies
Propitious seem; by song-birds led
The forest wafts us harmonies.

"'The passion-flowers round yonder tree
Have opened all their blossoms wide;
The bridal rose and *fleur de lis*,
And pinks that in the hedges hide.

"'Acacias, lindens, jessamines,
Smile on us with a gladsome air;
Myrtles, marjorams, eglantines,
White lilies, balm, and lavender.'

"'Yes,' said Felisa; 'but you see
Among them all lobelias grow,
The laurel, crown, and barberry,
Emblems of evil, scorn, and woe.

"'While in the sky appears a cloud,
A night-hawk screeches overhead,
So, knight,' and laughed she half aloud,
'I wonder when we two may wed?'

"'I see,' Andrino made reply,
'Thy meaning is that Nature will
Her kind approval ne'er deny
To him who wishes her no ill.

"'She frowns and smiles alike on all;
'Tis only he with mind morose,
Who, murmuring, finds the bitter gall
And takes, by choice, a noxious dose.

"'To all who hold a cheerful heart,
Each flower or shrub or tender blade
Is Providence, which doth impart
In turn bright sun or gladsome shade.

"'On good and bad the same rays fall,
And so to good or bad intent;
And what we have is not at all
More to us than to others sent.

"'What brings the bud to perfect bloom,
And breathes sweet life to hidden seed,
Sends blossoms to a darkened tomb
And proves the death of life, indeed.

"'According as we search, we find;
Enjoy as we appreciate,
So 'tis not Providence, but mind
That holds the keys of chance and fate.

"'This I believe, and now, dear one,
I see how Nature's winning smile
My joy increases with each sun,
And how things well my hours beguile.

"'But I am ready: give me this,
The charm thou hast, and let me go;
When I return most perfect peace
Shall crown what augured perfect woe.

"'And when the treasure—yours and mine—
I shall discover, we may wed,
Whether the earth with light doth shine
Or courts the storm-cloud overhead.'

"With clinging hand and fond caress,
Andrino left his love's abode,
And, in the somber wilderness,
Deep through its mystic shadows rode.

WITH TORTUOUS STRAITS AND STRANGE DEFILES
PASSING BETWEEN, DRAW EACH AND ALL

"Long was the ride, past jungles dense,
And swamp and plain and deep morass;
By Indian villages, and tents
Which sent their points up through the grass.

"Rivers he crossed, and muddy lakes,
In which dwelt things innumerable,
Lizards and toads and water-snakes
And beasts with coats invulnerable.

"Weary he grew as days went on,
But now at length drew near the shore,
Just as the light of early dawn
Tinged all the ocean o'er and o'er.

"And here he saw a myriad isles,
Narrow and wide and great and small,
With tortuous straits and strange defiles,
Passing between them each and all.

"Nor could he tell which one might be
The isle wherein the treasure lay;
And, blaming the temerity
That led him on so far away,

"Now off in spirit went the knight,
His body lying on the sand;
Through all the islands left and right,
And on the sea and on the land.

"Till came he to a lovely spot,
Shaded by royal trees of palm,
No better place could be, he thought,
For sweet repose and restful calm.

"'"Tis here,' said voices, 'we will touch
The utmost limit of our span,
Never in any age was such
A favor done for any man.

"'Not far art thou, good knight, from where
The treasure that thou seekest lies,
Which thou mayst find without a care,
If anxious, ere the daylight dies.'

"Then, as the knight awoke, his arm
Crossed heavy on a burdened breast,
He found the Spanish maiden's charm
Within his hand was tightly pressed.

"And to his mind the dream returned,
Nor, as he rose, did pass away;
'Come,' said he gaily, 'what is earned
'Must be secured without delay.'

"And so forthwith he made a boat
Of cypress trunk, hollow and large,
In which as swiftly could he float
Or safely, as in grander barge.

"Palmetto leaves for oars he took,
Yet scarcely needed oars at all,
For in this strange Elysian nook
Crowded were islands large and small

"So close the bark could guided be
On through the channels blue and still,
Slowly along or rapidly,
According to the boatman's will.

"Now came the morning rays, with light
Traversing all that sea of isles,
Turning the shadow frowns of night
Into the day's bright, laughing smiles.

"And morn laughed back, and dancing ray
Clove spears of gold through palm and fern,
As lone Andrino sought his way
With eager gaze, from bend to turn.

"At length he saw an island dark,
Which, to his eye, did surely seem,
As nearer drew he with his bark,
The very island of his dream.

"Tall, haughty palms grew high, and trees
Of other size and shade were there,
With blossoms sweet from which the bees
Bore their rich burdens through the air.

"Here stayed Andrino with his bark,
And drew it high upon the beach,
Far past the highest water mark,
Where tide and storm could never reach.

"And then Viola's letter took,
Reading it once again, to see
Where on the island he might look
If this the treasure spot should be.

"'The isle is small,' the letter said,
'Covered with tangle branch and vine;
But seek its center, thither led
Thy path will be by aid divine.'

"And so Andrino hurried fast,
Guided he knew not how, but still
On to the sought-for place, at last
By strange direction of some will.

"And there he saw, ah! must I say?
Fernando prone upon his face;
A lifeless, wasted form of clay,
Atoning for his past disgrace.

"Quite dead he lay across the mound
Of earth whereon no grasses grew,
And where, within deep underground,
Lay all the treasure he did sue.

"'Strange fate, alas!' Andrino mused,
'Has led my rival to this spot;
Without the charm he would have used
The very place his soul has sought.

"'And yet he knew it not, but died,
Miserable, starving, here alone.
God pity him! His virgin bride,
Must now his sins and hers atone.'

"Down in the white soil's hidden keep
Andrino found the maiden's gold;
And in its place, as far and deep,
Buried his rival in the mould.

"'*Quantum sufficit,*' carved he plain
In letters rude upon a cross;
'Since God alone can give the gain
'Tis right that he should send the loss.

"Full was Andrino's thankful heart,
When to his loving bride he went,
And found her willing then to start
For any shore or continent.

"Back to old Spain they sailed, and there
Were married into happy life;
No happier couple anywhere
Than Don Andrino and his wife.

"Not for themselves the gold they kept,
But gave it to the needy poor,
And many in their castle slept
Who sought admittance at their door.

"So, like a magic wreath around,
Good deeds and children circled them,
And, one by one, these gems were bound
Into a household diadem."

Here ended Dexter, as the camp-fire threw
Its dying glimmer on a sleepy crew,
And flashed and darkened like some lightning cloud,
While Tabler, soundly sleeping, snored aloud,
And thought the whole of this long tale he heard,
Hearing a sentence here, and there a word,
And flattered much himself that he could keep,
At this late hour, from falling fast asleep.
"Tell me some more," he said; "Fandrino will
The other fellow lord mos' surely kill,
Unless the captain of the ship they sail
Does lock the useless fellows both in jail."
"You have our thanks," said Benjamin; "but tell

Us what became of that false Spanish belle?"
"Yes," cried the others; "we are anxious all
To learn what to the maiden did befall."
"Little is known," said Dexter, "of her life
After Andrino married his sweet wife;
She left her native land and ne'er returned,
Nor where she went was ever surely learned;
Though some have said she crossed the sea, and came
Here to this land, disguised in dress and name,
And, much repenting of her former sin,
Tried by good deeds a better fame to win."
"My tale," cried Benjamin, "may only be
A sequel to the happy one, which we
Have gladly heard you tell, and this false maid
The same child to whose grave we homage paid."
"But so or not, good-night," we said to all,
And as we spoke
The fire's last embers darkened into smoke.

With this night ended all our trip as well,
For early in the morning it befell
That Tabler took a lonesome "spell,"
And said he would not go another mile
On sea or shore;
Nor with rich promises could we beguile
Or him implore.
"We've skipped across," said Tabler, "land and sea,
And, as the sayin' is, enough's enough for me;
We couldn't find no new thing now, you see:
A-hunting nothing arter finding it
Is like a-fighting arter you have fit;

Birds, flowers, and sech is good enough to see,
But something more substantial give to me."
We could not quell this mutiny, and so
Decided then, that very day, to go
  Back to our trees.
Besides, our clothes were old, for we
Had been a month or so at sea.
  Now came the breeze,
By whose kind help we sped along, nor took,
Like Lot's sad wife, a backward look.
Our shells we piled into the *Pet*,
And never did one thing forget
Of coral, sponge, of stones with color rare,
Of leaves and grasses gathered here and there,
Of alligator's teeth, and jaw of shark,
Of crabs, and claws, and moss, and weed, and bark,
Of birds, and nests, and eggs, and other things
Which Nature to this country kindly brings.
Thus laden now, we on our homeward way
Moved with the breeze through strait and stretching bay,
Camping by night upon some little isle,
And starting out before the morning's smile,
Till, when eight days had gone, on Tampa's shore
We furled our tattered sails and sailed no more.

iel Hawthorne, which author, by the way, was a near relative of Mr. Goodhue's grandfather. His family is an old one to which he refers with considerable pride. His ancestor, Wm. Goodhue, came to Massachusetts in 1636, and left a homestead still in possession of the Salem Goodhues. The family genealogy contains many well known names among which are those of "Gail Hamilton" (Miss Dodge) and Edna Dean Proctor.

Mr. Goodhue loves the South and the Southern people, as any one who reads his poetry need not be long in finding out. Many of his best sketches were written from notes taken in Virginia and North Carolina.

J. L. BROWN.

San Francisco, Cal.

. Brown, editor of the New Evening News, has bet $20, gainst $12,000, that Cleveland s New York State. That was ery best bet he could get.

NEWS NOTES.

last Sunday evening a darkey led the train at Bolling with k in his arms which appeared inhabited, and after examina- by several passengers it was vered to contain a real live an which he was trying to car- ith him as baggage, not having y enough to buy but one tick- Progressive Age.

e survey of the oyster waters ieutenant Francis Winslow, of United States Navy, is almost pleted. He was given six months in which to complete it, his years time having expired. The has been thoroughly well

ere is a picture of Durham and e is a lesson on its face; Statis of population: 1865, 60 inhab- s; 1870, 250 inhabitants; 188 0 inhabitants; 1884, 4,500 inhab ts: 1885, 5,767 inhabitants: esti-

A small boy some months ago stole horse and buggy and was incarcerated in prison, but because of his youth and the pleading of ignorance as to the guilt of the thing a man took him, when lo! before a month he had stolen another belonging to G. A. Evans.

The jury which Judge Graves ordered "out of the box" was as intelligen looking as any we have had for a long time and hence they feel indignant, and one of them has an able article in the Reflector vindicating himself and colleagues.

A,

Swan Quarter Items.

Cotton is opening rapidly.

Frost on the 1st morning of this month.

Rice crops are damaged but very little by the recent frosts.

Miss Pennie Farrow has taken charge of a school in Springfield, near Fairfield. Much success to her.

Miss Simmons, of Pantego, is visiting friends in our county. She is now the guest of Dr. O. S. Credle, of Lake Comfort.

Miss Mesella Gaskill has finished her school at Lake Forest. We are pleased to see all of our young teachers home

www.ingramcontent.com/pod-product-compliance
Lightning Source LLC
Chambersburg PA
CBHW030321270326
41926CB00010B/1461

* 9 7 8 3 7 4 4 6 5 2 1 1 7 *